George Barker was born in Ess poems was published by Faber and Faber in 1935, his *Collected Poems* in 1987, and his posthumous *Street Ballads* in 1992. After many years of living abroad, in Japan, America and Italy, he returned to England and lived in Norfolk until his death in October 1991.

Robert Fraser, who also edited George Barker's *Collected Poems*, is at present working on the poet's biography.

To George & Zdena
who have listened ~

Cass
6/21/1995

Poems (1935)
Calamiterror (1937)
Lament and Triumph (1940)
Eros in Dogma (1944)
The True Confession of George Barker, Book One (1950)
News of the World (1950)
A Vision of Beasts and Gods (1954)
The Seraphina (1958)
The View from a Blind I (1962)
The True Confession of George Barker, Book Two (1964)
Dreams of a Summer Night (1966)
The Golden Chains (1968)
Poems of Places and People (1971)
In Memory of David Archer (1973)
Dialogues, Etc. (1976)
Villa Stellar (1978)
Anno Domini (1983)
Collected Poems (1987)
Street Ballads (1992)

GEORGE BARKER

Selected Poems

*

edited by Robert Fraser

faber and faber

LONDON BOSTON

First published in 1995
by Faber and Faber Limited
3 Queen Square London WC1N 3AU

Photoset by Wilmaset Ltd, Wirral
Printed in England by Clays Ltd, St Ives plc

A CIP record for this book is available from the British
Library

ISBN 0–571–17285–7

Contents

Editor's Preface

Since the publication of his *Collected Poems* in 1987 the desire
has frequently been expressed for a volume of George Barker's
verse shorter in extent and more accessible to the public. It is
in response to this demand that, four years after the poet's
death, this selection is now offered. The endeavour, however,
has been to produce something other than a mere digest of the
Collected. A *Selected Poems* is an invitation to sample and to
appreciate, a significant *mêlée*, a box where sweets compacted
lie. Across the decades and the verse forms, poems call to one
another according to a system of elective affinities more
rigorous than time.

A sensitively organized *Selected* has to honour many claims.
There is, for example, the obligation to represent every kind of
poem: the lyrical, the occasional, the memorial, the jocular.
This is more especially the case with a poet such as Barker
who, from the moment of his recognition by Eliot at the age of
twenty-one, never ceased to experiment. Constantly moving
on, he achieved distinction in the sonnet, in the sestina, in the
ballade as well as in the varied species of free verse.
Throughout the same period he tried and projected many
voices behind all of which, forever re-expressed, lay an abiding
vision of the poet as one who, while responsible to his time,
evinces both the continuing consequences of our culpability
and the reviving possibilities of our innocence: that self-
renewing hope forever re-embodied in the child.

One must honour both the diversity and the consistency.
One must also reconcile the claims of chronology with
something more pressing: the composition of a satisfying
sequence. The solution I have adopted is to begin and end with
poems of a later date, and in between to suggest a
chronological drift within which late pieces are allowed to rub
shoulders with earlier ones. While mindful of chronology, I

have therefore attempted above all to bring before the reader the vocal presence of the poet, of what Barker once memorably called 'The Face Behind the Poem'.

I imagine a perfect and sympathetic setting: the shores of Lake Nemi, say, or the orangery of some fine country house. Gathered is a company of the most congenial and discriminating spirits: Sappho and Catullus, Addison, Lord Byron, A. E. Housman and W. H. Auden, together with one's favourite grandmother and six-year-old son. The evening is calm, the wine is poured. Before them through some felicitous necromancy is summoned the shade of George Barker (1913–91), who is invited to read his poems. The poet purses his lips. His right wrist is erect and quivers in the air. This is what you hear.

An expository introduction would be out of place in a compilation such as this. But for those seeking answers to inevitable questions, the date and source of each poem is given at its close. At the very beginning stands an essay of 1939, 'Therefore All Poems Are Elegies' which, it is hoped, may afford as helpful a point of entry into the later poetry as into the earlier.

Therefore All Poems Are Elegies

To be so closely caught up in the teeth of things that they kill you, no matter how infinitesimally kill you, is, truly, to be a poet: and to be a poet in fact it is additionally necessary that you should possess the tongues and instruments with which to record this series of infinitesimal deaths. And if, on top of this, you also possess the architectural intellect with which to erect a philosophy upon these experiences then you may recognize that to be alive means for the poet merely the following of this process of dying: so that at the last death, the one on a bed, only the finality of it will seem strange, and not the mechanics of it. This is the theology of poetry, the spiral of septenary death, each of whose circles creates the beatitude of a poem. And a word is as much an assassination as a poem is a memorial. So the poet, embroiled daily in his own decease, is caught in the toils of reality as profoundly and as hopelessly as the consumptive who drowns in his own saliva. I can give you the image of the captive of the Gaels, whose torture was to unwind his intestines around a tree: for this is the poet, whose bowels are wound round the Eden Tree in coils at once agonized: I mean each turn is a poem.

It is around the fundamental and impossible mystery of existence that the poet wraps his paroxysms; because he is the captive of his senses, who torture like the Gael. Every man avoids his death as long as he can and thus every poet writes the nicest rather than the best poems he can; for the best poems leave him so much more short of blood; but the nicest poems appearing much the same on the surface because the talented poet can camouflage them with technique, do not bleed him so deeply. This is one reason why Tennyson lived to be eighty. Blake, as a poet, died early, but hung about down here, an archangel who wrote what was, for a poet, not so much poetry as the dithyramb of the liberated spirit. I am not speaking so much of accidents such as the death of Keats, which obviously occurred *sub rosa*; I speak of such poets as Hopkins, with his ten year term of silence devoted to living rather than dying; of Swinburne, expert at composing the magnificent camouflage; Eliot, accidentally alive long after he died the first time, and Yeats, who demonstrably lived twice.

This consummation is not so devoutly wished that the poet will deliberately lock himself inside its Iron Virgin of Cologne. The skill in living, for the poet, is, as for the lover, to reach a paroxysm most often but at least expense of spirit. This is why Shakespeare wrote thirty-nine plays and why Chatterton wrote only one good poem: Chatterton simply did not know how to pair with the Muse who draws from you all she can.

For this reason the prospect of political accident cutting short the life appears as absurdly irrelevant. I am in the grip of a struggle which is far more terrible and far less noisy. I mean that between the creature who wants and yet does not want to kill himself daily for the sake of words, and the assassin who desires all the while that the word should not be spoken and the man should die: the personification of all those forces which contend with us to render us inarticulate in our misery and unremembered by our successors, the force of darkness on which we have inscribed our poems and our paintings and our songs and dances, our mathematics and our rituals of marriage and death: the force against which we spend our existence striving, who covers us up in the end with a mouthful of dirt, the force who whispers that a sin is a sin to terrify the mutations and permutations of the body as it lives. Against this Demogorgon the poet is Perseus who cannot win, but captures a head each time a poem is written. It is against this monster of eternal negation that I use the knife and scalpel of my hand and mind, and against no other. For there are greater mausoleums to make than those of the Unknown Warrior, there are the epics in which all action is preserved and honoured, the lyrics in which all emotions are immortalized, and the tragedies in which the perpetual tragedy is to be in part observed and enshrined.

Therefore all poems are elegies, and the real grief is the possibility of joy. So that I admire most of all those who sit in rooms and die. They are the martyrs to a darkness which is so much more formidable than fire. Which of us is one of them?

May 1939

At Thurgarton Church

To the memory of my father

At Thurgarton Church the sun
burns the winter clouds over
the gaunt Danish stone
and thatched reeds that cover
the barest chapel I know.

I could compare it with
the Norse longboats that bore
burning the body forth
in honour from the shore
of great fjords long ago.

The sky is red and cold
overhead, and three small
sturdy trees keep a hold
on the world and the stone wall
that encloses the dead below.

I enter and find I stand
in a great barn, bleak and bare.
Like ice the winter ghosts and
the white walls gleam and flare
and flame as the sun drops low.

And I see, then, that slowly
the December day has gone.
I stand in the silence, not wholly
believing I am alone.
Somehow I cannot go.

Then a small wind rose, and the trees
began to crackle and stir
and I watched the moon by degrees
ascend in the window till her
light cut a wing in the shadow.

I thought: the House of the Dead.
The dead moon inherits it.
And I seem in a sense to have died
as I rise from where I sit
and out into darkness go.

I know as I leave I shall pass
where Thurgarton's dead lie
at those old stones in the grass
under the cold moon's eye.
I see the old bones glow.

No, they do not sleep here
in the long holy night of
the serene soul, but keep here
a dark tenancy and the right of
rising up to go.

Here the owl and soul shriek with
the voice of the dead as they turn
on the polar spit and burn
without hope and seek with
out hope the holy home below.

Yet to them the mole and
mouse bring a wreath and a breath
of the flowering leaves of the soul, and
it is from the Tree of Death
the leaves of life grow.

The rain, the sometime summer
rain on a memory of roses
will fall lightly and come a-
mong them as it erases
summers so long ago.

And the voices of those
once so much loved will flitter
over the nettled rows
of graves, and the holly tree twitter
like friends they used to know.

And not far away the
icy and paralysed stream
has found it also, that day the
flesh became glass and a dream
with no where to go.

Haunting the December
fields their bitter lives
entreat us to remember
the lost spirit that grieves
over these fields like a scarecrow.

That grieves over all it ever
did and all, all not
done, that grieves over
its crosspurposed lot:
to know and not to know.

The masterless dog sits
outside the church door
with dereliction haunting its
heart that hankers for
the hand that it loved so.

Not in a small grave
outside the stone wall
will the love that it gave
ever be returned, not for all
time or tracks in the snow.

More mourned the death of the dog
than our bones ever shall
receive from the hand of god
this bone again, or all
that high hand could bestow.

As I stand by the porch
I believe that no one has heard
here in Thurgarton Church
a single veritable word
save the unspoken No.

The godfathered negative
that responds to our mistaken
incredulous and heartbroken
desire above all to live
as though things were not so.

Desire to live as though the
two-footed clay stood up
proud never to know the
tempests that rage in the cup
under a rainbow.

Desire above all to live
as though the soul was stone,
believing we cannot give
or love since we are alone
and always will be so.

That heartbroken desire
to live as though no light
ever set the seas on fire
and no sun burned at night
or Mercy walked to and fro.

The proud flesh cries: I am not
caught up in the great cloud
of my unknowing. But that
proud flesh has endowed
us with the cloud we know.

To this the unspoken No
of the dead god responds
and then the whirlwinds blow
over all things and beyond
and the dead mop and mow.

And there in the livid dust
and bones of death we search
until we find as we must
outside Thurgarton Church
only wild grasses blow.

I hear the old bone in me cry
and the dying spirit call:
I have forfeited all
and once and for all must die
and this is all that I know.

For now in a wild way we
know that justice is served
and that we die in the clay we
dread, desired, and deserved,
awaiting no Judgement Day.

(*Poems of Places and People*, 1971)

Street Ballad

Somewhere in the past there is a vacant room
    and there, on a bed of thorn
lies the one I should have been, who was
    never even born.

Haunted by all those things I should have been
    had I been him,
why does his innocence tear at my heart like wild
    flesh-eating cherubim?

(Street Ballads, 1992)

Ikons

To Edward

I

But was there time? No.
    There was never time.
There was only the breath
exhaled by the first burning
babe from a cloud, lasting
the whole of one flaming moment
before the ashes fell.

II

Where was the place? The place
    was not here.
Some far where else the
    celebration of bells,
    the house of sacred things,
the rider on the bull, the dying
    serpent's tears,
the peacock crying
and, like knives in the sky,
    extraordinary wings.

III

Can I come back to you?
    No one is there.
They are all gone. No one was
    ever there.
The mask of the holy man has
    faded now and

the silence is not golden.
    Through love shall we
labour to give birth to
    death, when the fiery
mountain and the inverted
    dog inherit the earth.

IV

Who was there? No one was
    ever there, where
the hands meet at midnight and
    the wave, breaking,
hangs for ever over
    rocks that cannot speak. There
you will find a face staring
    out of eyes
that cannot see the sea.

V

The leopard may sleep in chains
    and the nebula
bare a sunburst in its
    breast but
no dreams attend those cold
    lairs, no bone
grows from the grave there,
but sleeping, the gleam of the phoenix
    in the spread of its sunburst
dreams of old bones.

VI

And over October fields a single
    death stalks out of its life into
a river of subterranean springs.
    Haunted by knowledge it walks
into the lunar and erotic cave.
    And then the scarecrow speaks
of love to a ghost in the laurel grove.

VII

Whose blood drips from the engines? Whose?
    Overhead I hear the crack of
    February glass and the lightning
    dance in November coffins.
    Five loves
multiply zeros and crosses in the air
and where I seek you, find
wounds, only wounds with wings,
    wounds like knives.

VIII

Who are those apes sedulously
    re-setting type
that no one can ever read? Apples
    appear at the tips
of the god's fingers
    then deflate like bladders
because we know
    Laiki has always murdered
golden Apollo. These
    the images of eternal impermanence.

Whose was the voice? From
    far-off effigies
I hear the lyrics of
    those Grecian liars who
died for information.
    Will the table rise flapping
like an open book in the air
    and the alphabet, in a dance,
in a trance, continually declare
    the word is love, but there
is no word there.

Later the moon, rising over Russia
drew pyramidical constructions
    of white skulls out of
the steppes of the past, until I thought
I gazed upon philosophical battlements
dividing Europe and the hordes of bones
battling behind my eyes. Then
among those fallen I came upon my star.

The lesser mysteries always contain the greater
just as the zero multiplies or the circle
retreats into the recurring seven to leave us
wandering along a seacoast where Isaac Newton
    contemplating pebbles
takes by the arm a winged Victory that whispers:
    'Every one is everyone today.'

I have not learned the ceremonies of salvation
if they are not like this. They go,
the young dog dancing after old Adam,
and the flayed babe singing,
and Aphrodite, her belly full of cupids,
alighting tiptoe upon rocks,
all ceaselessly chanting in flames, ceaselessly chanting.

(*Street Ballads*, 1992)

Letter to a Young Poet

There is that whispering gallery where
A dark population of the air
Gives back to us those vocables
We dare not robe in syllables:

I speak of the whispering gallery
Of all Dionysian poetry
Within whose precincts I have heard
An apotheosis of the word

As down those echoing corridors
The Logos rode on a white horse;
Till every No that sense could express
Turned to a transcendental Yes.

Sanctified by such passages
Let us exchange our messages,
And, as we walk, all enigmas
Describe themselves in terms of stars.

From those lyrical waterfalls rise
Words that bring rainbows to the eyes
And memories called up from the ground
Smile to see their blood around.

There is a spirit of turbulence
Inhabiting the intelligence
Determined always to impose
Another reason on the rose

Another cause upon the creature
Than the privilege of its nature;
A handcuff and a history
Upon all natural mystery

And this turbulent spirit starts
That insurrection in our hearts
By which the laws of poetry
Are broken into anarchy:

The anarchy that seeks to show
An altitude which way to go,
Or use astronomy to prove
That duty is our only love.

But over the known world of things
The great poem folds its wings
And from a bloody breast will give
Even to those who disbelieve.

By the known world the intellect
Stands with its bright gun erect,
But the long loving verities
Are kissing at the lattices.

That dark population of the air
Leans downward, singing, to declare
The mystery of the world is this:
That we do not know what is.

(*A Vision of Beasts and Gods*, 1954)

Allegory of the Adolescent and the Adult

It was when weather was Arabian I went
Over the downs to Alton where winds were wounded
With flowers and swathed me with aroma, I walked
Like Saint Christopher Columbus through a sea's welter
Of gaudy ways looking for a wonder.

Who was I, who knows, no one when I started,
No more than the youth who takes longish strides,
Gay with a girl and obstreperous with strangers,
Fond of some songs, not usually stupid,
I ascend hills anticipating the strange.

Looking for a wonder I went on a Monday,
Meandering over the Alton down and moor;
When was it I went, an hour a year or more,
That Monday back, I cannot remember.
I only remember I went in a gay mood.

Hollyhock here and rock and rose there were,
I wound among them knowing they were no wonder;
And the bird with a worm and the fox in a wood
Went flying and flurrying in front, but I was
Wanting a worse wonder, a rarer one.

So I went on expecting miraculous catastrophe.
What is it, I whispered, shall I capture a creature
A woman for a wife, or find myself a king,
Sleep and awake to find Sleep is my kingdom?
How shall I know my marvel when it comes?

Then after long striding and striving I was where
I had so long longed to be, in the world's wind,
At the hill's top, with no more ground to wander
Excepting downward, and I had found no wonder.
Found only the sorrow that I had missed my marvel.

Then I remembered, was it the bird or worm,
The hollyhock, the flower or the strong rock,
Was it the mere dream of the man and woman
Made me a marvel? It was not. It was
when on the hilltop I stood in the world's wind.

The world is my wonder, where the wind
Wanders like wind, and where the rock is
Rock. And man and woman flesh on a dream.
I look from my hill with the woods behind,
And Time, a sea's chaos, below.

(*Lament and Triumph*, 1940)

Resolution of Dependence

We poets in our youth begin in gladness
But thereof come in the end despondency and madness.
Wordsworth, 'Resolution and Independence'

I encountered the crowd returning from amusements,
The Bournemouth Pavilion, or the marvellous gardens,
The Palace of Solace, the Empyrean Cinema: and saw
William Wordsworth was once, tawdrily conspicuous,
Obviously emulating the old man of the mountain-moor,
Traipsing along on the outskirts of the noisy crowd.

Remarkable I reflected that after all it is him.
The layers of time falling continually on Grasmere Churchyard,
The accumulation of year and year like calendar,
The acute superstition that Wordsworth is after all dead,
Should have succeeded in keeping him quiet and cold.
I resent the resurrection when I feel the updraft of fear.

But approaching me with a watch in his hand, he said:
'I fear you are early; I expected a man; I see
That already your private rebellion has been quelled.
Where are the violent gestures of the individualist?
I observe the absence of the erratic, the strange;
Where is the tulip, the rose, or the bird in hand?'

I had the heart to relate the loss of my charms,
The paradise pets I kept in my pocket, the bird,
The tulip trumpet, the penis water pistol;
I had the heart to have mourned them, but no word.
'I have done little reading,' I murmured, 'I have
Most of the time been trying to find an equation'.

He glanced over my shoulder at the evening promenade.
The passing people, like Saint Vitus, averted their eyes:
I saw his eyes like a bent pin searching for eyes
To grip and catch. 'It is a species,' he said,
'I feel I can hardly cope with – it is ghosts,
Trailing, like snails, an excrement of blood.

'I have passed my hand like a postman's into them;
The information I dropped in at once dropped out.'
'No,' I answered, 'they received your bouquet of daffodils,
They speak of your feeling for Nature even now.'
He glanced at his watch. I admired a face.
The town clock chimed like a cat in a well.

'Since the private rebellion, the personal turn,
Leads down to the river with the dead cat and dead dog,
Since the single act of protest like a foggy film
Looks like women bathing, the Irish Lakes, or Saint Vitus,
Susceptible of innumerable interpretations,
I can only advise a suicide or a resolution.'

'I can resolve,' I answered, 'if you can absolve.
Relieve me of my absurd and abysmal past.'
'I cannot relieve or absolve – the only absolution
Is final resolution to fix on the facts.
I mean more and less than Birth and Death; I also mean
The mechanical paraphernalia in between.

'Not you and not him, not me, but all of them.
It is the conspiracy of five hundred million
To keep alive and kick. This is the resolution,
To keep us alive and kicking with strength or joy.
The past's absolution is the present's resolution.
The equation is the interdependence of parts.'

(*Lament and Triumph*, 1940)

from Secular Elegies

I

My pig-faced kingdom with tongues of wrong
And an historical gait of trial and error,
Under whose bridges Time, faster than rivers,
Bears individual and event along
Into a past overloaded with souvenirs:

Now answer history with a marvellous golden Yes
As she steps up asking all future questions.
The historians in their tombs, sighing, will sleep
Deeper, and the sailors, who always had great visions,
Smile for the island that ceased to be an illusion.

The instinct of the bird governs its acts of war,
Who, titivating itself at crossroads, rises and rises
Singing from the destructive wheels that come roar-
ing towards it, and in the end, after the reverses,
Perches whistling on the shattered axles proudly.

The armies of Hohenzollern, brooding on loss,
Know best that the real enemy is never there
Pinned akimbo on the gun-sight, but in the cause.
O sheeted in their horoscopes like togas
Under red stars strut the catchpenny Caesars.

Heroes who ride your wishing horses over
The breakfast tables of the population,
Your beds are full of hands. And when you shiver
What stalks across your grave is a whole nation:
And when you close an eye your life is over.

But the conquerors, reddening their heels on us,
They will not ever really die, but continually
Thrash on the hotbed of their animus:
Not one of them shall die hopefully and finally,
For them the grave will also be full of us.

II

Where formerly he saw birds in bushes, now
The cyclist resting from his uphill labour
Observes the skull of Cromwell on a bough
Admonishing his half heart, and he shoulders
His way upward against the wind to the brow.

The political cartoonist in his bed
Hears voices break his sleep he does not know:
The morning papers show what the people said.
Librarians in their studies, the lights low,
Sense Milton breathing in his marble head.

The clerk hears Clive cheering in a darkness.
And from the ponds of commons, in broad day,
The effigies of great sailors rise in their starkness
With the *Hood* in their hands, and cry:
'Nevertheless we mourn also the *Bismarck*!'

There it is necessary to walk carefully
And swallows must dive wisely, for the air,
So full of poems and ghosts, is truly
Populated with more than meets the eye:
Some principles have become poltergeist there.

Where, in its sepulchres, the long past rests
Brocaded with daydreams, there the truth is known:
What makes the people happiest is best.
But the fish in its undersea caves and bird in its nest
Know that the shark and cuckoo never rest.

Sometimes the punts in summer on the rivers,
Gliding like dancers over the slovenly water
Saw as they traced their way among the shallows
Images under them pinned in a cage of shadows
Struggling to catch the eye. It was the future.

The quavering Chamberlain, trapped between disasters,
Hiding his head in an hour-glass: four kings and
The bicyclist Queen, like uprooted pilasters,
Flying across the sea: coiled in the ampersand
The hackencreuz accumulates but never masters.

And some, in silence, looking for their lives
In the lines of their hands, the merciless words saw
That turned Nebuchadnezzar into a cow:
Others, who came kissing and bringing olives,
Had a change of heart and are dead now.

Sad in his alcove of love Pascal lamented:
'My friend, my friend, you were born on the other side.'
Firstly we die because of places. O the demented
Alexander, who, eternally discontented,
Desires more, is us. Finally we die of pride.

Then from its labours I rest my hand on the table
And there where hitherto the poem had been,
Now, in its deadliness sleeping but capable,
Agent and gadget of destruction, the machine
Of actual damnation lies and is culpable.

Everything that we touch, sooner or later, –
The uprooted arbutus hung at the head of the bed,
The untouchable trophies in the arcanum of nature,
The dizzy stars, the testes, and the sacred
Dove – everything that we dissect for data
Dies as we finger for the heart of the matter.

O but the Doric arm tattooed with falsity
That riddles this embrace where worlds hide,
Larger than railways where they hold a country
Sleeping and waking in their iron anatomy,
Takes me to the breast where I am pacified

Under the frenzies of all sensual wonders.
What shall I say when, big at my mouth
The Hesperidean with a worm in its splendours
Hangs like the bub of a whore? Or what truth
Find in the kiss that dazzles all my windows?

And so in circles over existential deserts
I and you wander, lost, and arm in arm;
Lost, lost. And the visions paying us visits
Lead us to mirages where, in a morning dream,
We forget the headaches and the lost Edens.

Temper the whirlwind to the unborn lamb,
Mother of us all, lapped in your shawls of cause;
Large in your arms wrap our sad amalgam
That, spinning its tails among the other stars,
Mopes, lost and weeping, far, far from its home.

Cover with your pity the broken Pole
Where, like a rag, the pride of the human hangs
Dirty as dishcloths. And with summer console
Us for the equinox of our anguish.
Humour the arrogant ships that sail

Too near the tooth of the truth and the weather,
The thinkers in their cockleshells, the captains
Sinking each other; and always permit neither
Wholly to find their ends, for they seek islands
Of Death and Truth that should always be further.

And in due season to their last bed take
The lovers who are the cause of all the trouble;
Let the manikin Adam successfully undertake
What Atlas only, bending an apish double,
Hitherto managed with the world on his back.

O temper the whirlwind to the unborn lamb!
And on the tongue of the young in its cradle
Lightly lay silver spoons. And the same
Love extend to those who groom your bridal
That they, mother of us all, suffer in your name.

(*Eros in Dogma*, 1944)

To My Mother

Most near, most dear, most loved and most far,
Under the window where I often found her
Sitting as huge as Asia, seismic with laughter,
Gin and chicken helpless in her Irish hand,
Irresistible as Rabelais, but most tender for
The lame dogs and hurt birds that surround her, —
She is a procession no one can follow after
But be like a little dog following a brass band.

She will not glance up at the bomber, or condescend
To drop her gin and scuttle to a cellar,
But lean on the mahogany table like a mountain
Whom only faith can move, and so I send
O all my faith, and all my love to tell her
That she will move from mourning into morning.

(*Eros in Dogma*, 1944)

Summer Song I

I looked into my heart to write
  And found a desert there.
But when I looked again I heard
Howling and proud in every word
  The hyena despair.

Great summer sun, great summer sun,
  All loss burns in trophies;
And in the cold sheet of the sky
Lifelong the fish-lipped lovers lie
  Kissing catastrophes.

O loving garden where I lay
  When under the breasted tree
My son stood up behind my eyes
And groaned: Remember that the price
  Is vinegar for me.

Great summer sun, great summer sun,
  Turn back to the designer:
I would not be the one to start
The breaking day and the breaking heart
  For all the grief in China.

My one, my one, my only love,
  Hide, hide your face in a leaf,
And let the hot tear falling burn
The stupid heart that will not learn
  The everywhere of grief.

Great summer sun, great summer sun,
  Turn back to the never-never
Cloud-cuckoo, happy, far-off land
Where all the love is true love, and
  True love goes on for ever.

(*News of the World*, 1950)

Ode against St Cecilia's Day

Rise, underground sleepers, rise from the grave
    Under a broken hearted sky
And hear the swansinging nightmares grieve
    For this deserted anniversary
Where, horned, a hope sobs in the wilderness
    By the thunderbolt of the day.

Footfall echoing down the long ruin of midnight
    Knock like a heart in a box
Through the aural house and the sibylline skull
    Where once Cecilia shook her singing veils,
Echo and mourn. Footstepping word, attend her
    Where, here, bird of answer, she prevails.

Sleep, wormeaten weepers. Silence is her altar.
    To the drum of the head, muffled
In a dark time, the sigh is a hecatomb.
    Tender Cecilia silence. Silence is tender
As never a voice was. Here, dumb-
    Struck she mourns in the catacomb of her grandeur.

O stop the calling killer in the skull
    Like beasts we turn toward!
For was the nightriding siren beautiful
Caterwauling War until her bed was full
    Of the uxorious dead?
Let the great moaners of the seven seas
    Let only the seas mourn,
With the shipwrecked harp of creation on their knees
    Till Cecilia turns to a stone.

(*News of the World*, 1950)

Galway Bay

With the gulls' hysteria above me
I walked near these breakneck seas
This morning of mists, and saw them,
Tall the mysterious queens
Waltzing in on the broad
Ballroom of the Atlantic.

All veils and waterfalls and
Wailings of the distraught,
These effigies of grief moved
Like refugees over the water;
The icy empresses of the Atlantic
Rising to bring me omen.

These women woven of ocean
And sorrows, these far sea figures,
With the fish and skull in their
Vapour of faces, the icicles
Salting down from their eyelashes,
As I walked by the foreshore

Moved towards me, ululating:
O dragnet of the sweet heart
Bind us no longer! The cage
Bursts with passions and bones,
And every highspirited fish
Lives off our scuttled love!

I stood on a stone, the gulls
Crossed my vision with wings
And my hearing with caterwauling;
The hurdling wave, backbroken,
Died at my feet. Taller
Than the towering hour above me

The homing empresses of the sea
Came among me. And, shivering,
I felt death nuzzling in the nest
Of the diurnally shipwrecked
Drowned nocturnally breast.

(*News of the World*, 1950)

Verses for the Sixtieth Birthday of Thomas Stearns Eliot

I

By that evening window where
His accurate eye keeps Woburn Square
Under perpetual judgment so
That only the happy can come and go
About these gardens and not be
Tested in that dark neutrality,
Which, in between love and disgust,
Hates most of all its own mistrust,
I see this gentle and gothic man
Tame Apollyon with a pen.

II

I never know the juggernauts
Go bulldozing through my thoughts
So that everything I own
Is trod down and overthrown
Without remembering that worse
Than thunder in the hearse
Is the supernatural sigh
Of illusions as they die —
But in the rooms of Eliot
The visions whistle as they rot.

III

To him the dead twig in the gutter
Cries across all law to utter
Confidences that would bring
Tears to the eyes of anything.
But that set imperial face
Has looked down on our disgrace
And, without betraying so
Little as a twinge of sorrow,
Seen all grief begin again –
A gentle and long-suffering man.

IV

Outside the huge negations pass
Like whirlwinds writing on the grass
Inscriptions teaching us that all
The lessons are ephemeral;
But as the huge negations ride
And depredate all things outside
His window, he puts out his hand
And writes with whirlwinds on the ground
Asseverations that tame
The great negations with his name.

(*News of the World*, 1950)

To Charles Baudelaire

Walk with me, Sir, when nothing perpends
The wilderness within me. When I adhere
To the trumped up altar because I fear
An obscure answer, see that your ghost attends
Me, for what reason? Knowing I do not deserve
Vision or vigil of your serpent spirit
Untwined from knowledge to make me that visit,
Nevertheless I entreat. I serve
Much the same master. Was your good a god?
I hate my ruler because he will not break me
Under the overloving justice of his rod,
Thus but for love I hate him. Take me
To that inverted golgotha you trod
And, O Sir, show me the mirror that will break me!

(*News of the World*, 1950)

The True Confession of George Barker

Today, recovering from influenza,
  I begin, having nothing worse to do,
This autobiography that ends a
  Half of my life I'm glad I'm through.
O Love, what a bloody hullaballoo
  I look back at, shaken and sober,
When that intemperate life I view
  From this temperate October.

To nineteen hundred and forty-seven
  I pay the deepest of respects,
For during this year I was given
  Some insight into the other sex.
I was a victim, till forty-six,
  Of the rosy bed with bitches in it;
But now, in spite of all pretexts,
  I never sleep a single minute.

O fellow sailor on the tossing sea,
  O fleeting virgin in the night,
O privates, general in lechery,
  Shun, shun the bedroom like a blight:
Evade, O amorous acolyte,
  That pillow where your heart you bury –
For if the thing was stood upright
  It would become a cemetery.

I start with this apostrophe
   To all apostles of true love:
With your devotion visit me,
   Give me the glory of the dove
That dies of dereliction. Give
   True love to me, true love to me,
And in two shakes I will prove
   It's false to you and false to me.

Bright spawner, on your sandbank dwell
   Coldblooded as a plumber's pipe –
The procreatory ocean swell
   Warming, till they're overripe,
The cockles of your cold heart, will
   Teach us true love can instil
Temperature into any type.

Does not the oyster in its bed
   Open a yearning yoni when
The full moon passes overhead
   Feeling for pearls? O nothing, then,
Too low a form of life is, when
   Love, abandoning the cloister,
Can animate the bedded oyster,
   The spawning tiddler, and men.

Thus all of us, the pig and prince,
   The priest and the psychiatrist,
Owe everything to true love, since
   How the devil could we exist
If our parents had never kissed?
   All biographies, therefore,
– No matter what else they evince –
   Open, like prisons, with adore.

Remember, when you love another,
    Who demonstrably is a bitch,
Even Venus had a mother
    Whose love, like a silent aitch,
Incepted your erotic itch.
    Love, Love has the longest history,
For we can tell an ape his father
    Begot him on a mystery.

I, born in Essex thirty-four
    Essentially sexual years ago,
Stepped down, looked around, and saw
    I had been cast a little low
In the social register
    For the friends whom I now know.
Is a constable a mister?
    Bob's your uncle, even so.

Better men than I have wondered
    Why one's father could not see
That at one's birth he had blundered.
    His ill-chosen paternity
Embarrasses the fraternity
    Of one's friends who, living Huysmans,
Understandably have wondered
    At fatherhood permitted policemen.

So I, the son of an administer
    Of the facts of civil laws,
Delight in uncivil and even sinister
    Violations. Thus my cause
Is simply, friend, to hell with yours.
    In misdemeanours I was nourished –
Learnt, like altruists in Westminster,
    By what duplicities one flourished.

At five, but feeling rather young,
　With a blue eye beauty over six,
Hand in hand and tongue to tongue
　I took a sin upon my sex.
Sin? It was pleasure. So I told her.
　And ever since, persisting in
Concupiscences no bolder,
　My pleasure's been to undress sin.

What's the point of a confession
　If you have nothing to confess?
I follow the perjuring profession
　– O poet, lying to impress! –
But the beautiful lie in a beautiful dress
　Is the least heinous of my transgressions:
When a new one's added, 'O who was it?'
　Sigh the skeletons in my closet.

Ladybird, ladybird, come home, come home:
　Muse and mistress, wherever you are.
The evening is here and in the gloom
　Each bisexual worm burns like a star
And the love of man is crepuscular.
　In the day the world. But, at night, we,
Lonely on egos dark and far
　Apart as worlds, between sea and sea,

Yearn on each other as the stars hold
　One another in fields together.
O rose of all the world, enfold
　Each weeping worm against the cold
Of the bitter ego's weather:
　To warm our isothermal pride
Cause, sometimes, Love, another
　To keep us by an unselfish side.

The act of human procreation
    – The rutting tongue, the grunt and shudder,
The sweat, the reek of defecation,
    The cradle hanging by the bladder,
The scramble up the hairy ladder,
    And from the thumping bed of Time
Immortality, a white slime,
    Sucking at its mother's udder –

The act of human procreation
    – The sore dug plugging, the lugged-out bub,
The small man priming a lactation,
    The grunt, the drooping teat, the rub
Of gum and dug, the slobbing kiss:
    Behold the mater amabilis,
Sow with a saviour, messiah and cow,
    Virgin and piglet, son and sow? –

The act of human procreation,
    – O crown and flower, O culmination
Of perfect love throughout creation –
    What can I compare to it?
O eternal butterflies in the belly,
    O trembling of the heavenly jelly,
O miracle of birth! Really
    We are excreted, like shit.

II

The Church, mediatrix between heaven
   And human fallibility,
Reminds us that the age of seven
   Inaugurates the Reason we
Spend our prolonged seniority
   Transgressing. Of that time I wish
I could recount a better story
   Than finding a shilling and a fish.

But Memory flirts with seven veils
   Peekabooing the accidental;
And what the devil it all entails
   Only Sigmund Freud suspects.
I think my shilling and my fish
   Symbolized a hidden wish
To sublimate these two affects:
   Money is nice and so is sex.

The Angel of Reason, descending
   On my seven-year-old head
Inscribed this sentence by my bed:
   The pleasure of money is unending
But sex satisfied is sex dead.
   I tested to see if sex died
But, all my effort notwithstanding,
   Have never found it satisfied.

Abacus of Reason, you have been
    The instrument of my abuse,
The North Star I have never seen,
    The trick for which I have no use:
The Reason, gadget of schoolmasters,
    Pimp of the spirit, the smart aleck,
Proud engineer of disasters,
    I see phallic: you, cephalic.

Happy those early days when I
    Attended an elementary school
Where seven hundred infant lives
    Flittered like gadflies on the stool
(We discovered that contraceptives
    Blown up like balloons, could fly);
We memorized the Golden Rule:
    Lie, lie, lie, lie.

For God's sake, Barker. This is enough
    Regurgitated obscenities,
Whimsicalities and such stuff.
    Where's the ineffable mystery,
The affiancing to affinities
    Of the young poet? The history
Of an evolving mind's love
    For the miseries and the humanities?

The sulking and son-loving Muse
    Grabbed me when I was nine. She saw
It was a question of self-abuse
    Or verses. I tossed off reams before
I cared to recognize their purpose.
    While other urchins were blowing up toads
With pipes of straw stuck in the arse,
    So was I, but I also wrote odes.

There was a priest, a priest, a priest,
    A Reverend of the Oratory,
Who taught me history. At least
    He taught me the best part of his story.
Fat Father William, have you ceased
    To lead boys up the narrow path
Through the doors of the Turkish Bath?
    I hope you're warm in Purgatory.

And in the yard of the tenement
– The Samuel Lewis Trust – I played
While my father, for the rent
    (Ten bob a week and seldom paid),
Trudged London for a job. I went
    Skedaddling up the scanty years,
My learning, like the rent, in arrears,
    But sometimes making the grade.

O boring kids! In spite of Freud
    I find my childhood recollections
Much duller now than when I enjoyed
    It. The whistling affections,
All fitting wrong, toy railway sections
    Running in circles. Cruel as cats
Even the lower beasts avoid
    These inhumanitarian brats.

Since the Age of Reason's seven
    And most of one's friends over eight,
Therefore they're reasonable? Even
    Sensible Stearns or simpleton Stephen
Wouldn't claim that. I contemplate
    A world which, at crucial instants,
Surrenders to adulterant infants
    The adult onus to think straight.

At the bottom of this murky well
   My childhood, like a climbing root,
Nursed in dirt the simple cell
   That pays itself this sour tribute.
Track any poet to a beginning
   And in a dark room you discover
A little boy intent on sinning
   With an etymological lover.

I peopled my youth with the pulchritude
   Of hetaerae noun-anatomized;
The literature that I prized
   Was anything to do with the nude
Spirit of creative art
   Who whispered to me: 'Don't be queasy.
Simply write about a tart
   And there she is. The rest's easy.'

And thus, incepted in congenial
   Feebleness of moral power
I became a poet. Venial
   As a human misdemeanour,
Still, it gave me, prisoner
   In my lack of character,
Pig to the Circean Muse's honour.
   Her honour? Why, it's lying on her.

Dowered, invested and endowed
   With every frailty is the poet –
Yielding to wickedness because
   How the hell else can he know it?
The tempted poet must be allowed
   All ethical latitude. His small flaws
Bring home to him, in sweet breaches,
   The moral self-indulgence teaches.

Where was I? Running, so to speak,
    To the adolescent seed? I
Found my will power rather weak
    And my appetites rather greedy
About the year of the General Strike,
    So I struck, as it were, myself:
Refused to do anything whatsoever, like
    Exercise books on a shelf.

Do Youth and Innocence prevail
    Over that cloudcuckoo clime
Where the seasons never fail
    And the clocks forget the time?
Where the peaks of the sublime
    Crown every thought; where every vale
Has its phantasy and phantasm
    And every midnight its orgasm?

I mooned into my fourteenth year
    Through a world pronouncing harsh
Judgements I could not quite hear
    About my verse, my young moustache
And my bad habits. In Battersea Park
    I almost heard strangers gossip
About my poems, almost remark
    The bush of knowledge on my lip.

Golden Calf, Golden Calf, where are you now
    Who lowed so mournfully in the dense
Arcana of my adolescence?
    No later anguish of bull or cow
Could ever be compared with half
    The misery of the amorous calf
Moonstruck in moonshine. How could I know
    You can't couple Love with any sense?

Poignant as a swallowed knife,
    Abstracted as a mannequin,
Remote as music, touchy as skin,
    Apotheosizing life
Into an apocalypse,
    Young Love, taking Grief to wife,
And tasting the bitterness of her lips,
    Forgets it comes from swabbing gin.

The veils descend. The unknown figure
    Is sheeted in the indecencies
Of shame and boils. The nose gets bigger.
    The private parts, haired like a trigger,
Cock at a dream. The infant cries
    Abandoned in its discarded larva,
Out of which steps, with bloodshot eyes,
    The man, the man, crying Ave, Ave!

III

That Frenchman really had the trick
    Of figure skating in this stanza:
But I, thank God, cannot read Gallic
    And so escape his influenza.
Above my head his rhetoric
    Asks emulation. I do not answer.
It is as though I had not heard
    Because I cannot speak a word.

But I invoke him, dirty dog,
    As one barker to another:
Lift over me your clever leg,
    Teach me, you snail-swallowing frog,
To make out of a spot of bother
    Verses that shall catalogue
Every exaggerated human claim,
    Every exaggerated human aim.

I entreat you, frank villain,
    Get up out of your bed of dirt
And guide my hand. You are still an
    Irreprehensible expert
At telling Truth she's telling lies.
    Get up, liar; get up, cheat,
Look the bitch square in the eyes
    And you'll see what I entreat.

We share, frog, much the same well.
    I sense your larger spectre down
Here among the social swill
    Moving at ease beside my own
And the muckrakers I have known.
    No, not the magnitude I claim
That makes your shade loom like a tall
    Memorial but the type's the same.

You murdered with a knife, but I
    Like someone out of Oscar Wilde
Commemorate with a child
    The smiling victims as they die
Slewing in kisses and the lie
    Of generation. But we both killed.
I rob the grave you glorify,
    You glorify where I defiled.

O most adult adulterer
  Preside, now, coldly, over
My writing hand, as to it crowd
  The images of those unreal years
That, like a curtain, seem to stir
  Guiltily over what they cover –
Those unreal years, dreamshot and proud,
  When the vision first appears.

The unveiled vision of all things
  Walking towards us as we stand
And giving us, in either hand,
  The knowledge that the world brings
To those her most beloved, those
  Who, when she strikes with her wings
Stand rooted, turned into a rose
  By terrestrial understandings.

Come, sulking woman, bare as water,
  Dazzle me now as you dazzled me
When, blinded by your nudity,
  I saw the sex of the intellect,
The idea of the beautiful.
  The beautiful to which I, later,
Gave only mistrust and neglect,
  The idea no dishonour can annul.

Vanquished aviatrix, descend
  Again, long-vanished vision whom
I have not known so long, assume
  Your former bright prerogative,
Illuminate, guide and attend
  Me now. O living vision, give
The grave, the verity; and send
  The spell that makes the poem live.

I sent a letter to my love
    In an envelope of stone,
And in between the letters ran
A crying torrent that began
To grow till it was bigger than
Nyanza or the heart of man.
I sent a letter to my love
    In an envelope of stone.

I sent a present to my love
    In a black-bordered box,
A clock that beats a time of tears
As the stricken midnight nears
And my love weeps as she hears
The armageddon of the years.
I sent my love the present
    In a black-bordered box.

I sent a liar to my love
    With his hands full of roses
But she shook her yellow and curled
Curled and yellow hair and cried
The rose is dead of all the world
Since my only love has lied.
I sent a liar to my love
    With roses in his hands.

I sent a daughter to my love
    In a painted cradle.
She took her up at her left breast
And rocked her to a mothered rest
Singing a song that what is best
Loves and loves and forgets the rest.
I sent a daughter to my love
    In a painted cradle.

I sent a letter to my love
    on a sheet of stone.
She looked down and as she read
She shook her yellow hair and said
Now he sleeps alone instead
Of many a lie in many a bed.
I sent a letter to my love
    On a sheet of stone.

O long-haired virgin by my tree
    Among whose forks hung enraged
A sexual passion not assuaged
    By you, its victim – knee to knee,
Locked sweating in the muscled dark
    Lovers, as new as we were, spill
The child on grass in Richmond Park,
    The cemetery of Richmond Hill.

Crying the calf runs wild among
    Hills of the heart are memories:
Long long the white kiss of the young
    Rides the lip and only dies
When the whole man stalks among
    The crosses where remorse lies –
Then, then the vultures on the tongue
    Rule empires of white memories.

Legendary water, where, within
    Gazing, my own face I perceive,
How can my self-disgust believe
    This was my angel at seventeen?
Stars, stars and the world, seen
    Untouched by crystal. Retrieve
The morning star what culprit can
    Who knows his blood spins in between?

Move backward, loving rover, over
    All those unfeathered instances
I tar with kiss of pitch, the dirty
    Lip-service that a jaded thirty
Renders its early innocences.
    Pointer of recollection, show
The deaths in feather that now cover
    The tarry spot I died below.

What sickening snot-engendered bastard
    Likes making an idiot of himself?
I wish to heaven I had mastered
    The art of living like a dastard
While still admiring oneself.
    About my doings, past and recent,
I hear Disgust — my better half —
    'His only decency's indecent.'

Star-fingered shepherdess of Sleep
    Come, pacify regret, remorse;
And let the suffering black sheep
    Weep on the bed it made. Let pause
The orphic criminal to perceive
    That in the venue of his days
All the crimes look back and grieve
    Over lies no grief allays.

Sleep at my side again, my bride,
    As on our marriage bed you turned
Into a flowering bush that burned
    All the proud flesh away. Beside
Me now, you, shade of my departed
    Broken, abandoned bride, lie still,
And I shall hold you close until
    Even our ghosts are broken-hearted.

So trusting, innocent, and unknowing
   What the hazards of the world
Storm and strike a marriage with,
   We did not hear the grinders blowing
But sailed our kisses round the world
   Ignorant of monsters and the vaster
Cemetery of innocence. This wreath
   Dreams over our common disaster.

But bright that nuptial to me now
   As when, the smiling foetus carried
Rose-decked today instead of tomorrow,
   Like country cousins we were married
By the pretty bullying embryo
   And you, my friend: I will not borrow
Again the serge suit that I carried
   Through honey of moon to sup of sorrow.

Loving the hand, gentle the reproving;
   Loving the heart, deeper the understanding;
Deeper the understanding, larger the confiding
   For the hurt heart's hiding.
Forgiving the hand, love without an ending
   Walks back on water; giving and taking
Both sides become by simple comprehending:
   Deeper the love, greater the heart at breaking.

IV

O Bishop Andrewes, Bishop Berkeley,
  John Peale Bishop and Bishop's Park,
I look through my ego darkly
  But all that I perceive is dark:
Episcopally illuminate
  My parochial testaments
And with your vestal vested vestments
  Tenderly invest my state.

Let Grace, like lace, descend upon me
  And dignify my wingless shoulder:
Let Grace, like space, lie heavy on me
  And make me seem a little older,
A little nobler; let Grace sidle
  Into my shameful bed, and, curling
About me in a psychic bridal,
  Prove that even Grace is a darling.

The moon is graceful in the sky,
  The bird is graceful in the air,
The girl is graceful too, so why
  The devil should I ever care
Capitulating to despair?
  Since Grace is clearly everywhere
And I am either here or there
  I'm pretty sure I've got my share.

Grace whom no man ever held,
   Whose breast no human hand has pressed,
Grace no lover has undressed
   Because she's naked as a beast –
Grace will either gild or geld.
   Sweet Grace abounding into bed
Jumps to it hot as a springald –
   After a brief prayer is said.

Come to me, Grace, and I will take
   You close into my wicked hands,
And when you come, make no mistake,
   I'll disgrace you at both ends.
We'll grace all long throughout the night
   And as the morning star looks in
And blanches at the state we're in –
   We'll grace again to be polite.

For Marriage is a state of grace.
   So many mutual sacrifices
Infallibly induce a peace
   Past understanding or high prices.
So many forgivenesses for so many
   Double crossings and double dealings –
I know that the married cannot have any
   But the most unselfish feelings.

But the wise Church, contemplating
   The unnatural demands
That marriage and the art of mating
   Make on egoists, commands
We recognize as sacramental
   A union otherwise destined
To break in every anarchic wind
   Broken by the temperamental.

Off the Tarpeian, for high treason,
    Tied in a bag with a snake and a cock,
The traitor trod the Roman rock.
    But in the bag, for a better reason,
The married lovers, cock and snake,
    Lie on a Mount of Venus. Traitor
Each to each, fake kissing fake,
    So punished by a betrayed creator.

'The willing union of two lives.'
    This is, the Lords of Justice tell us,
The purpose of the connubial knot.
    But I can think of only one
Function that at best contrives
    To join the jealous with the jealous,
And what this function joins is not
    Lives, but the erogenous zone.

I see the young bride move among
    The nine-month trophies of her pride,
And though she is not really young
    And only virtually a bride,
She knows her beauties now belong
    With every other treasure of her
Past and future, to her lover:
    But her babies work out wrong.

I see the bridegroom in his splendour
    Rolling like an unbridalled stallion,
Handsome, powerful and tender,
    And passionate as an Italian –
And nothing I could say would lend a
    Shock of more surprise and pride
Than if I said that this rapscallion
    Was necking with his legal bride.

I knew a beautiful courtesan
  Who, after service, would unbosom
Her prettier memories, like blossom,
  At the feet of the weary man:
'I'm such a sensitive protoplasm,'
  She whispered, when I was not there,
'That I experience an orgasm
  If I *touch* a millionaire.'

Lying with, about, upon,
  Everything and everyone,
Every happy little wife
  Miscegenates once in a life,
And every pardonable groom
  Needs, sometimes, a change of womb,
Because, although damnation may be,
  Society needs every baby.

It takes a sacrament to keep
  Any man and woman together:
Birds of a forgivable feather
  Always flock and buck together:
And in our forgivable sleep
  What birdwatcher will know whether
God Almighty sees we keep
  Religiously to one another?

I have often wondered what method
  Governed the heavenly mind when
It made as audience to God
  The sycophant, the seaman sod,
The solipsist – in short, men.
  Even the circus-stepping mare
Lifts her nose into the air
  In the presence of this paragon.

For half a dozen simple years
    We lived happily, so to speak,
On twenty-seven shillings a week;
    And, when worried and in tears,
My mercenary wife complained
    That we could not afford our marriage,
'It's twice as much,' I explained,
    'As MacNeice pays for his garage.'

I entertained the Marxian whore –
    I am concerned with economics,
And naturally felt that more
    Thought should be given to our stomachs.
But when I let my fancy dwell
    On anything below the heart,
I found my thoughts, and hands as well,
    Resting upon some private part.

I sat one morning on the can
    That served us for a lavatory
Composing some laudatory
    Verses on the state of man:
My wife called from the kitchen dresser:
    'There's someone here from Japan.
He wants you out there. As Professor.
    Oh, yes. The War just began.'

So Providence engineered her
    Circumstantial enigmas,
And the crown of the objector
    Was snatched from me. In wars
The conscientious protester
    Preserves, as worlds sink to force,
The dignified particular.
    Particularly one, of course.

'The hackneyed roll call of chronology' –
    Thus autobiography to de Quincey.
And I can understand it, since he
    Lived like a footnote to philology.
But the archangelic enumeration
    Of unpredictable hejiras –
These, with a little exaggeration,
    I can adduce for my admirers.

And so, when I saw you, nightmare island,
    Fade into the autumnal night,
I felt the tears rise up for my land,
    But somehow these tears were not quite
As sick as when my belly laughed
    Remembering England had given me
The unconditional liberty
    To do a job for which I starved.

v

Almighty God, by whose ill will
    I was created with conscience;
By whose merciful malevolence
    I shall be sustained until
My afflictions fulfil
    His victories; by whose dispensation
Whatever I have had of sense
    Has obfuscated my salvation –

Good God, grant that, in reviewing
   My past life, I may remember
Everything I did worth doing
   Seemed rather wicked in pursuing:
Grant, Good God, I shall have remitted
   Those earthly pleasures beyond number
I necessarily omitted,
   Exhausted by the ones committed.

Good God, let me recollect
   Your many mercies, tall and short,
The blousy blondes, the often necked,
   And those whom I should not have thought
Given wisely to me; nor let forget
   My grateful memory the odd
Consolers, too frequently brunette,
   Who charged me for your mercies, God.

Good God, let me so recall
   My grave omissions and commissions
That I may repent them all,
   – The places, faces and positions;
Together with the few additions
   A feeble future may instal.
Good God, only mathematicians
   Consider Love an ordinal.

Good God, so wisely you provided
   The loving heart I suffer with,
That I am constantly divided
   By a deep love for all beneath
Me. Every man knows well
   He rides his own whores down to hell,
But, good God, every knackered horse
   Was, originally, yours.

Good God, receive my thanksgiving
    For all the wonders I have seen
(And all the blunders in between)
    In my thirty-odd years of living.
I have seen the morning rise
    And I have seen the evening set —
Anything different would surprise
    Me even more profoundly yet.

Good God, receive my gratitude
    For favours undeserved: accept
This truly heartfelt platitude:
    You gave me too much latitude
And so I hanged myself. I kept
    Your mercy, Good God, in a box
But out at midnight Justice crept
    And axed me with a paradox.

O living kindness of the knife
    That cuts the proud flesh from the rotten
Ego and cuts the rotten life
    Out of the rotten bone! No, not an
Ounce of sparrow is forgotten
    As that butchering surgeon cuts
And rummages among my guts
    To succour what was misbegotten.

I confess, my God, this lonely
    Derelict of a night, when I
And not the conscious I only
    Feel all the responsibility —
(But the simple and final fact
    That we are better than we act,
For this fortunate windfall
    We are not responsible at all) —

I confess, my God, that in
    The hotbed of the monkey sin
I saw you through a guilt of hair
    Standing lonely as a mourner
Silent in the bedroom corner
    Knowing you need not be there:
I saw the genetic man had torn a
    Face away from your despair.

I confess, my God, my Good,
    I have not wholly understood
The nature of our holiness:
    The striking snake errs even less
Not questioning; the physicist
    Not asking why all things exist
Serves better than those who advance a
    Question to which life's the answer.

But, O my God, the human purpose,
    If at all I can perceive
A purpose in the life I live,
    Is to hide in the glass horse
Of our doubt until the pity
    Of heaven opens up a city
Of absolute belief to us,
    Because our silence is hideous

And our doubt more miserable
    Than certainty of the worst would be.
Like infinitely pitiable
    Ghosts who do not even know
They waver between reality
    And unreality, we go
About our lives and cannot see
    Even why we suffer so.

I know only that the heart
  Doubting every real thing else
Does not doubt the voice that tells
  Us that we suffer. The hard part
At the dead centre of the soul
  Is an age of frozen grief
No vernal equinox of relief
  Can mitigate, and no love console.

Then, O my God, by the hand
  This star-wondered grief takes
The world that does not understand
  Its own miseries and mistakes
And leads it home. Not yet, but later
  To lean an expiated head
On the shoulder of a creator
  Who knows where all troubles lead.

VI

I looked into my heart to write.
  In that red sepulchre of lies
I saw that all man cherishes
  Goes proud, rots and perishes
Till through that red room pitiless night
  Trails only knife-tongued memories
To whose rags cling, shrieking, bright
  Unborn and aborted glories.

And vinegar the mirages
    That, moaning they were possible
Charge me with the unholy No.
    The unaccomplished issue rages
Round the ringed heart like a bull
    Bellowing for birth. But even so
Remorselessly the clock builds ages
    Over its lifeless embryo.

Ruined empire of dissipated time,
    Perverted aim, abused desire,
The monstrous amoeba cannot aspire
    But sinks down into the cold slime
Of Eden as Ego. It is enough
    To sink back in the primal mud
Of the first person. For what could
    Equal the paradise of Self-love?

The necessary angel is
    The lie. Behind us, all tongues splayed,
The lie triumphant and tremendous
    Shields us from what we are afraid
Of seeing when we turn – the Abyss
    Giving back a face of small
Twisted fear – and this is all,
    To conquer the lie, that we possess.

Come, corybantic self-delusion,
    And whisper such deceptions to
Me now that I will not care who
    Or what you are, save palliation
Of the question-marked heart. Let rest
    The harp and horror horned head upon
That green regenerative breast
    By whose great law we still live on.

Now from my window looking down
    I see the lives of those for whom
My love has still a little room
    Go suffering by. I see my own
Stopped, like a stair carpet, at this story
    Not worth the telling. O memory
Let the gilded images of joys known
    Return, and be consolatory!

Bitter and broken as the morning
    Valentine climbs the glaciered sky
With a spike in his foot. The lover's warning
    Blazes a sunrise on our misery:
Look down, look down, and see our grey
    And loveless rendezvous, Valentine:
Fold, then, in grief and cast away
    The love that is not yours or mine.

On this day of innocent
    And happy lovers, let me praise
The grotesque bestiary of those
    Who love too much. Monsters invent
Monsters, like babies that gypsies raise
    In odd bottles for freak shows –
These love too deeply for the skin.
    Whose bottle are you monster in?

The grotesque bestiary where
    Coiled the pythoness of sighs,
To keep a beast within her there
    Crushes him in her clutch of vice
Till, misshapen to her passion, dead,
    The lion of the heart survives
By suffering kisses into knives
    And a spiked pit into a bed.

Stand in your sad and golden-haired
    Accusation about me now,
My sweet seven misled into life.
    O had the hotheaded seaman spared
Those breast-baring ova on their bough,
    There'd be no aviary of my grief,
No sweet seven standing up in sorrow
    Uttering songs of joy declared.

Of joy declared, as birds extol
    The principle of natural pleasure
Not knowing why. Declare to all
    Who disbelieve it, that delight
Naturally inhabits the soul.
    I look down at you to assure
My sense of wrong: but you declare
    Whatever multiplies is right.

I looked into my heart to write.
    But when I saw that cesspit twisted
With the disgusted laws that live
    In royal domination under
The surface of our love, that writhe
    Among our prizes, they attested
The putrefaction of our love
    Spoils the spawner of its grandeur.

VII

Today the twenty-sixth of February,
   I, halfway to the minute through
The only life I want to know,
   Intend to end this rather dreary
Joke of an autobiography.
    Thirty-five years is quite enough
Of one's own company. I grow
   A bit sick of the terrestrial stuff

And the celestial nonsense. Swill
   Guzzle and copulate and guzzle
And copulate and swill until
   You break up like a jigsaw puzzle
Shattered with smiling. The idiotic
   Beatitude of the sow in summer
Conceals a gibbering neurotic
   Sowing hot oats to get warmer.

Look on your handwork, Adam, now
   As I on mine, and do not weep.
The detritus is us. But how
   Could you and I ever hope to keep
That glittering sibyl bright who first
   Confided to us, perfect, once,
The difference between the best and the worst?
   That vision is our innocence.

But we shall step into our grave
   Not utterly divested of
The innocence our nativity
   Embodies a god in. O bear,
Inheritors, all that you have,
   The sense of good, with much care
Through the dirty street of life
   And the gutter of our indignity.

I sense the trembling in my hand
   Of that which will not ever lower
Its bright and pineal eye and wing
   To any irony, nor surrender
The dominion of my understanding
   To that Apollyonic power
Which, like the midnight whispering
   Sea, surrounds us with dark splendour.

Enisled and visionary, mad,
   Alive in the catacomb of the heart,
O lonely diviner, lovely diviner, impart
   The knowledge of the good and the bad
To us in our need. Emblazon
   Our instincts upon your illumination
So that the rot's revealed, and the reason
   Shown crucified upon our desolation.

You, all whom I coldly took
   And hid my head and horns among,
Shall go caterwauling down with me
   Like a frenzy of chained doves. For, look!
We wailing ride down eternity
   Tongue-tied together. We belong
To those with whom we shook the suck
   And dared an antichrist to be.

Get rags, get rags, all angels, all
  Laws, all principles, all deities,
Get rags, come down and suffocate
  The orphan in its flaming cradle,
Snuff the game and the candle, for our state
  – Insufferable among mysteries –
Makes the worms weep. Abate, abate
  Your justice. Execute us with mercies!

(*The True Confession of George Barker*, Book One, 1950)

'Turn on your side and bear the day to me'

Turn on your side and bear the day to me
Beloved, sceptre-struck, immured
In the glass wall of sleep. Slowly
Uncloud the borealis of your eye
And show your iceberg secrets, your midnight prizes
To the green-eyed world and to me. Sin
Coils upward into thin air when you awaken
And again morning announces amnesty over
The serpent-kingdomed bed. Your mother
Watched with as dove an eye the unforgivable night
Sigh backward into innocence when you
Set a bright monument in her amorous sea.
Look down, Undine, on the trident that struck
Sons from the rock of vanity. Turn in the world
Sceptre-struck, spellbound, beloved,
Turn in the world and bear the day to me.

(*News of the World*, 1950)

Memorial Inscription

O Leopardi! O Lion-pawed Seas!
Give tongue, give tongue, against, again
The mistress of all miseries
The master of all mysteries
O Lion-pawed heart! O voices of stone!
Shatter the tabernacle in which we grieve,
Crack the mad jacket in which we rejoice
   Alive for ever alone!

(News of the World, 1950)

Goodman Jacksin and the Angel

ANGEL

Thus, Goodman Jacksin, time has come
For truth in cockleshells and nuts;
I beg you leave your head and home,
Come, cut the cackle, (cackle cuts)
And to the catchpenny cosmos show
The vipers nuzzling in your guts
And my tall spectres shaped of snow.

JACKSIN

What, get down off the five-barred star
To let a bullying gale blow in?
I know what kind of a rogue you are,
When I step out, you will step in.
There are no matters, to my mind,
Worth any labour in the mouthing:
I'll just sit here on my behind –
All your wind amounts to nothing.

ANGEL

Look, Farmer Cynic, chips are down.
The scarecrows howl about the hills,
Clocks gaze in crystals, fishes drown,
It's more than a cold wind that kills.
O bullyboy, leave the two-headed self
To peep both ways with a knowing leer;
The world is still your better half,
And it's not somewhere else – it's here.

JACKSIN

I'm not the man for you, my stranger.
I've got my hands quite full enough.
I bow my head at my soul's anger
And when I've got a cold I cough.
Leave well, that's me, leave well alone.
Why come to pester us with these
Cold questions set too near the bone?
What's it to me if angels freeze?

ANGEL

What's it if this sanctuary,
The holy of the holy heart
Where, paraclete in an aviary,
The mind beatifies every part
That goes to make a singing soul –
What's it to you if this bright temple
Is split in two from pole to pole?
Well, what's an earthquake, for example?

JACKSIN

With these bright eyes I have witnessed
What the bright ploughshare also sees;
The running generations harnessed
In green laws to divine decrees:
The seeding generations under
Every winter solstice stir,
And, from the earth at a dead end,
A daughter rise up, praising her.

ANGEL

My Goodman Jacksin, for this prize,
This curious privilege of dirt,
You, man of clay, yes, bright of eyes,
Are but responsible in part.
A very little part. You lay
Your rag and bone down in a grave
To fructify dirt in a way –
But this is all the part you have.

JACKSIN

Angelic Cynic, sing to me
Of all my greater purposes –
Apocalypse I die to see,
That allegory that always is
Rising up through obscurities
To dazzle my bright eyes:
O revelation of verities
Whose loving never dies.

ANGEL

What abstract crackpot could so love
You, Goodman Jacksin, straw in hair,
You, with all pigeons and no dove,
You Monday hound and Sunday hare,
You, axing oracles with a fact –
With you, part mud and three parts water,
What heavenly vision, now or later,
The rainbow covenant will contract?

JACKSIN

I tell you, Angel, that gods die,
Princes and gross empires pass,
But the bright stars of heaven shall
Rotate for ever in my arse.
The hand that turns the zodiac
In its great circle over all,
Is the horned fist of a husband jack
With a bright eye on the ball.

ANGEL

Honouring itself the clay rears up
To praise its pottering purposes,
But, oh, much sorrow shall it sup
Before fulfilment is.
That Dagon slumbers in every seed
Who shall rise up and rend,
Then you shall need a friend indeed
But find a fiend instead.

JACKSIN

I wake on mornings in the winter
With the holy snow on the ground,
I see the hoofmarks milling round
Where nightlong in the cattle pound
I and the cloven fiend, hellbound,
Wrestle together, without a sound,
For the white world that sleeps around
As we rage in the centre.

ANGEL

The rooftops bear his sinning track!
His goat-hooves outrage bed and birth!
O draw the sheet over the earth –
I see the horn begin to jack
Against all daughters of innocence!
O Goodman Jacksin, underneath
The sweet dream and the simple sense,
His hunting semen ferrets death.

JACKSIN

You rave like any soapbox gabber.
Evil is simply this, my friend:
A good we do not understand.
Right at the heart of all this blabber
The good is matching with the bad,
But which is which, O angel-demon,
What final proof was ever had?
What's the issue of your semen?

ANGEL

At the living centre of all this,
Evil and good, in expiation,
Dovetail the great antithesis
As they clasp round the ends of creation:
As when, in winter, through a window,
A sad man sees the sun endow
The skeleton of his private sorrow
A bedizening transfiguration.

JACKSIN

You, Jew jumped up from an ilex tree,
Who gave you this heartburn of laurels?
An old man whom I cannot see,
A fathering farmer of farrows,
With his blackjack spade, a gun on his knee,
And his everlasting quarrels: —
I like my money no more than he
Loves his pocketful of morals.

ANGEL

You see your youngest son at dawn
Stalk out into eerie mist,
A strapping strider, a man born
An Adam from the first: —
But darkly in the devoted mind
You dog him from his chancy cradle
In dread that, laid out on a hurdle,
He will come back — to the ground.

Jehovah also saw you stride
Out of a green and guarded gate
Into the mystery of your fate:
He too felt the crossbone shadow ride
The stalking horse of his heart,
As, tracking, anxious, secret, saw
The hounds of hell rout out and start
All the sorrow you were born for.

JACKSIN

Red, red the daybreak when I rose
To find I was the son
Of that far loving father whose
Son is as sad as my own.
I would not have the half of my grief
Put upon beast or god,
No, leave to me the best belief:
My sorrow is the greatest.

ANGEL

Goodman Jacksin, Jacksin Goodman,
You burn the twisted auburn leaves,
Thinking, like any other woodman,
'The leaves are like ourselves.'
The splintered glitter of the dead,
And the falling heroes of melancholy,
Do they not serve, in her holy bed,
The mother of all that is holy?

JACKSIN

O crystal and snow-hearted eagle
Inhabit the hills of my soul
So that I too, like a sexless angel,
May see things from a better angle
And lose the heart in the whole,
Not in the cellar of a single
Consecration but nailed out
On the vast edges of all doubt.

ANGEL

The androgynous worm and I
Your guardian arable and green,
Like caryatids hold up between
Us all oppositions under the sky.
Seraphic I take to my breast
The basilisk spirallings of the lie,
Only to find I rock to rest
The dove in a dichotomy.

JACKSIN

The adultress shall have such sweet dreams
That the babe in her arms will smile:
As, by apparent accident,
Evolving through the obscure schemes
Of our spiritual systems,
Obvious Evil, as it seems,
Emerges, in a little while,
Redeemed, and white, and provident.

ANGEL

The laws of act and consequence
Obey a justice none
May follow with a rational sense –
For it is not our own.
Odylic engines of destiny
Who can say what will come
From the venially inserted penny –
What Juggernauts roll in time?

JACKSIN

I watch boys chasing butterflies
Among the summer hedges:
I hear their high and hunting cries
As the sky-blown flier dodges
Between their hands, till, in disguise
Against the dog-rose lodges
Then they stand silent by the rose
To see a rainbow close its wings.

ANGEL

And out of the horn rumpled sheet
Where nightlong in their forking lock
The hissing kissers slew and mock
That image from which they were cast –
Out of that fouled and rocking nest
In which those justly outcast meet
And mount like stray dogs in the street, –
Out, out the innocent image steps.

JACKSIN

O Minotaur! A maze! A maze!
We only know what we have done
And through what hecatombs have been
When, there before us, we come upon
Bleeding our crying footprints run
Across, ahead. And we have seen
The lost tracks, like a fugitive son,
Of some long forgotten cause.

ANGEL

The falling feather can engender
By no known laws of heredity
A generation of clashing rocks:
And conceptions of great spiritual splendour
Derive, through successions of paradox,
From brief moments of cheap misery;
Just as the flat and selfish sea
Has set a crowned amoeba free.

JACKSIN

Or sewing the sweet thistledown sigh
Reap whirlwinds in a daughter womb,
And never know whose exiled cry
Unlooses on us, worlds away,
This avalanche of vinculum
As, idle in a drawing room,
We watch the goldfinch prisoner die
As this silent ghost goes by.

ANGEL

So, ruddy husbandman, foot of clay,
I too am a dog's demigod,
And tell you, majesty of mud,
That neither you nor I can say
Where the first fault really lay.
But all those living creatures who
Inherit, just because they live,
The property of error – O forgive!

JACKSIN

Come, petty parson, that's much better.
But let me butt in with a word:
I'm not the postman with a black letter,
I'm not the vengeance of the Lord
Engaged in some small-time vendetta –
Come, tell me, which of us, in truth,
Could ever really forgive the other?
And who could ever forgive us both?

ANGEL

My guilt shines in the glittering
Perennial and praying tree,
That, without dropping on its knee,
Praises never flattering.
The shame of angels is their love
Must so abase itself before
That hallelujah they adore, –
Has more idolatry than love.

JACKSIN

And yet what can we do if we are
Swept up in such a storm of wings
As that authoritative power –
What do save cower in our fear?
Then in that bosomed and huge cave
Crouch, trusting that our cooing love
Declare in fear and tremblings:
We are crushed out by that thunder?

ANGEL

O let the shivering leaf disclose
The susurrus of that solicitude
Not stirs the feather on a wren
But cools the rotors of the stars.
That giant sleeps in molecules
And exercises in iotas
The earthquake of his regimen
On pismires of all magnitude.

JACKSIN

I saw the spawning fishes write
My guilt shine on the water's bed;
Yes, too much love, like you, my friend,
I also gave; but O to what?
Not the landlord of the infinite,
(So deeply in his debt I stand)
But to all living things instead
We give the love that is not ours.

ANGEL

She shakes the winged horse in his stall
For her you break your roots and walk
Water to clasp snakes and trees;
All living things obey her: all
Support each other for their own sake.
Then as, on those maternal knees,
Sit sucking at that happy milk,
Forget a father got all these.

JACKSIN

Thus the antinomy of love
Inverts its propositions. We
– Fourteen stone and an Idea –
Turned tables turtle truly have.
The sibyl trudges through my mud
To show me her humility,
And I trapeze on a dizzy cloud
To teach Azrafel not to fear.

ANGEL

In the arched dialectic by
Which all existence must evolve,
There is no wallflower at the dance,
On all things that first law devolves.
And thus the innocent must die
Because its very innocence
By law of opposition calls
The skulls to lead it in that dance.

JACKSIN

There is no mystery in this
A man and women do not know:
The law of dialectics is
How Love evolves. There are no
Two ones of any kind but must
Bring forth a firstborn third to prove
That the arithmetic of love
Transcends our lonely dust.

ANGEL

Thus Love and Death together got
Under a dark constellation,
And in their fever they forgot
That even Love and Death are not
Exempt from generation.
Then from their open-eyed embrace
Rose the first god that ever was,
With doom in his face.

JACKSIN

How shall I speak of mystery
With a gun and a pound in my hand?
I must obey a master I
Shall never understand.
All flesh is grass, all grass is flesh
And the midnight sun roars down:
I and my soul go up in a flash,
I and my soul go down.

(*A Vision of Beasts and Gods*, 1954)

Roman Poem I

Why is this lake so sacred? It is sacred
    Because it is still.
Such a stillness is holy, for, unlike a river
    Or even the sea
Those huge mythologies endemic overhead
    May, without a lie,
Behold themselves here as they truly believe
    The gods to be.
Shown in the drowning heavens of Albano
    Would they rather
Sleep in its deeper altitudes than the sky?
    Sometimes a feather
From them descends on to the evening surface
    To take upon
Itself the curve and veer of that faint sail
    Leaning for haven
Over Albano. Or a small fish may rise
    Seeking to leap
Into the mackerel patterning of their wings
    And dying eyes.
Holy Albano, I have seen the low storm
    Saunter more slowly
Over your font and prism, as its form
    Immersed in so
Lucid a peace received a christening grace:
    Or perhaps more
Slowly moved over not to vex that still face
    With a dragging shower.
    Birds in your air

Loiter like visiting hierophants who hope
    To steal from the place
Some miraculous touch. So I, too, this day
    Having further come
And for as brief a slaking at this lake
    In spiritual expiation,
Having a little refreshed in your lustrations
    What may be saved
Of jaded nature, I too take away
    From your holy springs
The evanescent absolution of water.

Roman Poem II

A SHOWER IN ROME

The rain flickering here on this lonely day
   Over the brown roofs of Rome
Calls to my mind I am not so far away
   From my own house and home.
But then I hear the old clay within me cry
   Every man is in Coventry
And to the dirt his day is exiled from
   Must sometime come.

The shower sweeps westward to Ostia
   Like a plane trailing
A trembling net of rain, and on the far
   Landscape toiling
Armies of cloud climb and fall and are
   Gone. At once the air
Sunbursts with radiance like a shattered ceiling
   Dazzling everywhere.

— 82 —

Everywhere save here in the vaults of the heart
   Where no sun can
Delve to the bloodstained urn — so dark a part
   Of the unhouselled man
That only a gnashing of death can penetrate
   From all those also immured
In the life long home. Interred in its fate
   Bone howls to be heard.

But nevertheless above, like birds with rain,
   The hands of circumstance
Unwind my blinding sheets and, once again
   I feel the spirit dance
Up from its unholy cave, and regain
   That illumination once
Unhaunted by the bell and clappered presence
   Of human degradation.

Down in its pits the triumph of the Tarquin
   Regales those smiling dead
Just as though human delight could win
   Life instead
Back from the damp tomb and the last bed.
   Sexual joy within
These muddy tenements lifts up its head
   To begin, for ever, again.

And caged in rock beside the Capitol
   Padding her twenty foot track
The mother of Rome, loping up and back,
   Smiles as the bullies howl
Proudly: Lupe! at that imperial
   Bitch on the prowl —
The pride of a creature that has never died
   Crowns her, and her whole pack.

A bed of roses and a wreath of bay
    Birds of a shower, bear
Down to these tarnished demigods of clay –
    Triumph is here
To aggrandize with the trophies and regalia
    Of our crossed victories,
Or to degrade, as with a snivelling shower,
    The Ænean glories.

Roman Poem III

A SPARROW'S FEATHER

There was this empty birdcage in the garden.
    And in it, to amuse myself, I had hung
pseudo-Oriental birds constructed of
    glass and tin bits and paper, that squeaked sadly
as the wind sometimes disturbed them. Suspended
    in melancholy disillusion they sang
of things that had never happened, and never
    could in that cage of artificial existence.
The twittering of these instruments lamenting
    their absent lives resembled threnodies
torn from a falling harp, till the cage filled with
    engineered regret like moonshining cobwebs
as these constructions grieved over not existing.
    The children fed them with flowers. A sudden gust
and without sound lifelessly one would die
    scattered in scraps like debris. The wire doors
always hung open, against their improbable
    transfiguration into, say, chaffinches
or even more colourful birds. Myself I found
    the whole game charming, let alone the children.

And then, one morning – I do not record a
   matter of cosmic proportions, I assure you,
not an event to flutter the Volscian dovecotes –
   there, askew among those constructed images
like a lost soul electing to die in Rome,
   its feverish eye transfixed, both wings fractured,
lay – I assure you, Catullus – a young sparrow.
   Not long for this world, so heavily breathing
one might have supposed this cage his destination
   after labouring past seas and holy skies
whence, death not being known there, he had flown.
   Of course, there was nothing to do. The children
brought breadcrumbs, brought water, brought tears in their
   eyes perhaps to restore him, that shivering panic
of useless feathers, that tongue-tied little gossip,
   that lying flyer. So there, among its gods
that moaned and whistled in a little wind,
   flapping their paper anatomies like windmills,
wheeling and bowing dutifully to the
   divine intervention of a child's forefinger,
there, at rest and at peace among its monstrous
   idols, the little bird died. And, for my part,
I hope the whole unimportant affair is
   quickly forgotten. The analogies are too trite.

(*The View from a Blind I*, 1962)

At the Birth of a Child

For Raffaella-Flora

Sacred fountain, let me find
at the genesis of our kind
some consolation of the mind.

On this dark November morning
the aureola of the dawn
like a golden child is born

so this day takes its origin
from impulses that begin
beyond the star we suffer in

and the babe steps from a cloud
where, before the heart's endowed
with all that's miserable, or proud,

there all creatures fraternize
and find in one another's eyes
the innocence that always dies.

This is that welcome of the stars
the lost and drowning sailor hears
like angels whistling at his ears

or the weeping caryatid
bowing down its heavy head
burdened with what it never did:

in the astrologies of night
they see that death is growing bright
with stars that never reach our sight.

And the cherubs of the day
redeem in their sacred play
the nightmare of our Succubae

as the infant of the breast
brings to those who cannot rest
the peace we had thought dispossessed.

It is the death of innocence
the cherubim of birth announce
on the trumpets of existence.

(*Dreams of a Summer Night*, 1966)

from Dreams of a Summer Night

I

What was the date of that day when, unbefriended by any
Of those who had preceded us, without advice from the gods,
Who sulked as usual in their tents of vanity,
Cold and not wholly convinced of the purpose of our journey
We set out for whatever it is we find at the end of the day?
And why should that date matter? It matters because the rogation
Of all ceremonial knows, when it reaches full circle
Then its purpose is done, as when the praying wheel slowly
Rides to its point of rest with a last supplicatory sigh.
I do not know the purpose of this journey, or even
If in the end it reaches a purpose, and have no desire to know, for
                                                    the prospects
Are so wholly marvellous in themselves that to contemplate
Them is enough. The little house on the mountain
Where a hero was born with a ploughshare in his left fist and
A new word for love in his mouth, the painted and shallow
                                        springs of the Umbrian
Who loved white oxen, the ruined sea-palace of a black king
Visible only to angels and aeroplanes and the incurious rainbow-
                                                            fish,
And, O Calabria, those white beehive small farmsteads
To which, as it seems, the dignity of man has at last retreated
Awaiting another defeat: such an enumeration
Of almost sacred instances is always a personal litany
And enough is enough for the day. Thus in the evening
We know that whatever has happened may, in itself, comprise
The complete supplication. And the sigh
Of the heart as it closes its blowzy old rose for the night could
Well be the smile of the holy wheel as it comes to rest.

III

When the majority looks out of its moral citadel
Does it smile upon us, we whom it knows to be only
The oddfellow gardeners, the slightly drunken eccentrics with
Manias about outmoded machinery like honour,
The mutual duty of creatures afraid of each other to
Forgive what they fear, and an obsession with loneliness?
To this giant of majority whose home is a cave
In which hang the hearts, the hands, the dreaming heads
Of those victims whose sacrifice, like caryatids, supports the
                                                    citadel,
To this Polyphemus what shall we answer, save in a whisper,
'No man.' And the scapegoat, weeping huge tears in the wilderness,
Turns and looks backward upon the scenes of its childhood
Knowing only too well that though it believed it was once
Loved in its own home, it never, no never, was.
So too in derelict allotments one hears the crying, the shouting
Of those children who do not know that they are begging
Among the fallen ceilings and the broken beer bottles and the debris
For a hand to gather them and a step to lead them home to
The sacred hearth. And then, as I hear them, I remember
That Polyphemus is us, and the sad monster who rages
Weeping in his cave and wilderness, outcast, pariah,
Rejected, the ontological scapegoat of destiny,
Tossing the twisted horns of those morals upon which it is tossed,
This Prometheus of majority, this giant whispering on the fiery
                                                    rocks,

Cries out at last to a greater monster with one eye:
'O Everyman.'

IV

From whom save those who sleep in a strange cloud beside us —
The acanthus entwining their limbs like heart-leafed involvements
                                                    and the
Promise bruising their parted lips as they breathe it so lightly
That the butterflies alighted on their eyelids never even
So much as stir — from whom save them can we always
Evoke the forgiveness that exacts even more torment?
I am brought to these effigies that dream at the Tomb of Pompey
By that path through the park where, in the evening rain,
I walked with a friend in November, and saw, under the trees
Shadowed and silhouetted in the patterned moonlight,
Spellbound, the lovers. Then the raincloud suddenly
Obscured the moon, and in the rain and the darkness
I heard the moaning of those who are so hopelessly chained
                                                    together
That they walk in each other's dreams, and, in torment together,
Cry out in a hideous joy as they burn to ashes
Like the bird in the fable of fire. For the head of Pompey, dreaming
In those serene gardens set between lakes and a sea,
Forgets as it mourns that all it has lost is the mystical
Body of loving and of suffering.

IX

I saw this villa set in a garden of arbours and bowers
Of immense decaying roses and a grapevine long untended;
Tall weeds had invaded the paths and, hanging by rusty nails
The trellis work, broken, seemed to regret a hand that was gone.
                                                    There
By a half-open french window, standing in a white trance of silence
I saw one whom I loved cradling asleep in her arms
One whom I loved, and though no chill wind shuddered
The decaying roses or clattered the broken shutters,

Though no bough stirred,
Though no tall weed hissed and no grapevine trembled,
I knew that a zephyr of death had entered that garden
And that no one else would ever enter that garden.

XI

To find that the house really stands there under tall trees
With a field and a small bridge to the right and, to the left,
Where, as I knew it would be, the walled garden of peaches
Never closes its old door to intruder or visitor, there
I came at last upon the house that I knew was truly the past.
On the lawn the old colonel and his lady sat, she with a book and
He dozing in a deckchair with a shabby cocker spaniel beside him
And all their dead friends standing with teacups in their hands
Around them, recalling those summers long gone before emperors
Retired into libraries and the heroic goldenhaired soldiers
All died in that dirty valley of passion. Do the gods look down
On this little tea party taking place in the daydreams of
An ageing colonel as he dozes in a later August
And whisper: 'Yes, we were wrong'? Some of the dead who
Stood chatting in groups on the lawn in their outmoded
And beautiful finery seemed to know that in death a
Splendour invested them which no life could ever
Ever have imparted to them, that their destiny was hereafter to
Stroll on a terrible stage in a dumbshow perpetuating
Their otherwise fated, their fleeting, their almost forgotten
Memory. Admonished by these spectres we remember.

As I approached the Colonel stood up and extended his hand to me
Out of the past, and I held it not briefly, knowing that
Sometimes, but only too seldom, we can take tea with the dead.

The shades of childhood
Rise before me
Turning away their
Forgotten faces
But still I see
Like a glass of tears
The eyes of childhood
Gaze upon me.

Why do they turn
Away from me
Every wild one of
My shades of childhood?
Each seems to see
The ghost of its conscience
Like a white presence
Standing by me.

Then who tell me who
Ah who are they
The forgotten faces
Mopping and mowing
In Time like a tree?
Foretelling foreknowing
All the sad stories
That are now the memories
Of what had to be.

Is it I or you
O shades of childhood
I hear mourning in
Time like a tree?
O angel shades
Rise up and cover
Our eyes so that we
Cannot see.

Never no never
Ever return to
That wild wood
Where like larks
We once rose and sang
O shades of childhood
Crowd now around me
As here in my heart our
Shadows hang.

I hear them sighing
Like voices that fade
When the song is over
As shade after shade
Falls away from me:
O shades of childhood
Farewell for ever.
Remember me. O
Remember me!

Those dreams of Medusa's head hung there in the hand of the hero
Who shall reveal them? 'I was the housedog petrified in its
Pompeiian convulsion, I was the babe born in the hotbed of the
                                                    Abomination
And the ship howling in darkness and the anarchic sea
Cropfull of hands. I was the pitiless regard of heaven
Turned upon these things with never a tear mystifying
Its indifferent eyes. I was my shadow smiling up from Death Valley
                                                    and
Hypnotized, chanting a paean in praise of destruction,
Death, dereliction, destruction. I was the City of London in flames
                                    with, overhead, virgins
Plucking their psalteries and saints contemplating their navels.
I was the engines of Justice rusting in the skies of sunset
And armies asleep dreaming of peace. I was tempests
Gathering in thunderheads over the heart's red sea and
Ah, I was lightning dividing it.' Agonized head of Medusa
Greater degradations await you, the keys uncrossed and the
                                                    flaming
Gates that prevail as Armageddon uncoils from its sleep
And instead of the sun a dragon of hydrogen rises up in the Orient.
Thus I take you, dreaming head, in my hands where you lie
Cast away by the hero, rejected by anthropologists, discarded
By all save those who eavesdrop on your nightmare,
And lift your whispering death's-head from the floorboards
Of my small room here in Islington. I gaze into the still
Living and petrifying eyes and kiss the chill
Grave of your lips. I hear you, as in a dream, Medusa, moan:
'I am the sorrow that turns the heart to stone,'

(*Dreams of a Summer Night*, 1966)

Morning in Norfolk

As it has for so long
come wind and all weather
the house glimmers among
the mists of a little
river that splinters, it
seems, a landscape of
winter dreams. In the far
fields stand a few
bare trees decorating
those mists like the fanned
patterns of Georgian
skylights. The home land
of any heart persists
there, suffused with
memories and mists not
quite concealing the
identities and lost
lives of those loved once
but loved most. They haunt it
still. To the watermeadows
that lie by the heart they
return as do flocks of swallows
to the fields they have known
and flickered and flown so
often and so unforgettably over.
What fish
play in the bright wishing
wells of your painted
stretches, O secret
untainted little Bure,
I could easily tell,
for would they not be

those flashing dashers
and sometimes glittering
presentiments, images
and idealizations
of what had to be?
The dawn has brightened the
shallows and shadows and
the Bure sidles and idles
through weed isles and fallen
willows, and under
Itteringham Mill, and
there is a kind of rain-
drenched flittering in the
air, the night swan still
sleeps in her wings and over it all
the dawn heaps up the hanging
fire of the day.

Fowell's tractor blusters
out of its shed and drags
a day's work, like a piled sled
behind it. The crimson
December morning brims over
Norfolk, turning
to burning Turner
this aqueous water colour
idyll that earlier gleamed
so green that it seemed
drowned. What further
sanction, what blessing
can the man of heart intercede for
than the supreme remission
of dawn? For then the mind
looking backward upon its

too sullied yesterday,
that rotting stack of
resolution and refuse,
reads in the rainbowed sky
a greater covenant,
the tremendous pronouncement:
the day forgives.

Holy the heart in
its proper occupation
praising and appraising this
godsend, the dawn.
Will you lift up your eyes
my blind spirit and see
such evidence of
forgiveness in the heavens
morning after golden
morning that even
the blind can see?

(*Poems of Places and People*, 1971)

from In Memory of David Archer

To lift a hand
to those who have gone before us
those friends and
oddfellows to whom
only death can restore us
(I have heard
as in day dreams
them calling sometimes for us
out of a silence that seems
like a dead chorus)
to lift a hand in farewell
for them at the black bell
neither you David nor I
found this a hard thing to do –
for they, most of them, died
in a sort of twisted pride
or as they lifted up
the whiskey in the cup
or turning a handsome head
in honour among the dead
so that, with the wave
of a hand toward the grave
you and I, as they went
down out of the present,
could seem to call:
'Stand up and speak well
in the empty hall
of heaven or empty hell
for us all.'
But, David, I am at

such a loss, such a loss
that I cannot, I can not
lift a hand or a word
as you descend
the under ground
and one way stair
to that dead end
where
the friend is found.
Are you there
now? Dear friend
it does not matter where
you are for better or
worse where you are
there can be there
no more of the withering
belief (O withering arm
and withering leaf!)
or the withering Upas tree
of life,
no more ever again
of that pain.
The decent dirt
David unlike the lovers
will not desert you nor
the grave stone hurt
you but with love convert
you into stone, into
the dust and earth
of which both life and death
know the worth.
The dark streets at night
echoing our tread
seem for a moment bright

with what we said
and what we might
even have done, but the light
or dream of those times
is gone
and it was not done.
The familiar vision faded
and is forgotten in
our failure, so degraded
that ideal by
our delusion, so humiliated
we by what we knew
was both foregone and fated,
that in the end
what you saw, my friend,
was that life itself
was the vision
that you hated.
All the gifts of red
roses and blank
cheques and bed
fellows grew rank
and went bad
and you and they
sank down in the grey
ends of a day
that stank as it died
in the guttering
palace. I think
that all you leave
behind you in the evening
is a darkened room
empty save for old
newspapers and cigarette ends

and in the gloom
the enormous gold
urn of your heart
in which lie the ashes of your friends.

VIII

I cannot see. The place I do not know.
Who is that person standing by the wall?
Why do you ask the date on which I died?
Where is the house to which I am asked to go?
What was the question you put to me when
I happened to be listening to that child
Crying for god knows what outside the door?
Who is it calling me again and again
From my own chamber like a person lost?

I hear the dead man calling from the desert
But never the love, never the love, never.
I saw you. I saw you there. You were the other
Side of that window always hidden in shadow.
I cannot see. The place is not the place where
I was supposed to be. Who are those people
Whispering, with heads together, in the corner?
Why do they speak when they should be silent?

I think that I see, walking in the moonlight
The Magus Zoroaster and my dead father
Talking together. What is this heartbroken
House? Is this my home? Why do you look at me
As though I had no parents? Who is at the window?
You? It is you? I saw you pass, your hand
Covering your face in shadow, and, in the moonlight,
Falling, seven wounds, like stars.

IX

I hear the children crying in the infanticidal night
I hear the wild wind blowing till it blows the cold moon white
I see morning gathering up the leaves to bury them from sight
And the doves and Mercy silent in the forest.

Where were you Lamp that always burns within the darkest wood?
The Parson said: What happens always happens for the good.
There, looking on with winter eyes, the Will of God just stood
And the doves and Mercy silent in the forest.

Where were you Christian Andersen? Or Mary, where were you
When these two babes together lay down and the cold wind blew?
The Will of God, that cold cold wind, blew through them through
                                   & through,
And the doves and Mercy silent in the forest.

These little ones, these pretty ones, they're luckier than most.
And now not even fate can find these two forever lost
Beside a bush beneath a tree covered with snow and frost,
And the doves and Mercy silent in the forest.

XXXVII

In the evening in the basement my brother and I,
as had become our practice, took out the foils and
after a few flourishes began to fence. He retreated
slowly, smiling, up the three stone steps. I said:
Ah like a character in an opera and advanced.
He continued to smile. I drove the sword forward and saw
very slowly, as one perceives an enormous natural calamity,
the unguarded point of my foil enter his right eye.
And then all motions ascended into a reality
where they occurred with a kind of paralysed and
yet exaggerated formality, like slow motion automata.

I remember that my right hand lowered the foil
and I saw my brother's right eye hanging out on
the sixteen-year-old bone of his cheek. I heard his
blade rattle on the stone floor of the basement. I saw
the remaining eye of his face stare at me as though
I was not there. He placed his
right hand on the iron railing and raised
his left hand to the gap in his face from which
lachrymal fluid and blood exuded like grape juice.
I think that we stood thus, without speech or movement,
for several years. And as I stood staring
at the half blind person I loved most of all
with his optical nerve hooked out and his young
hand resting on the rail, I felt the gorgon's head
rising within my own so that I could not see.
Upon this motionless scene like a Revenger's play
set upon a staircase, as though she must have known
what it was that she had always been destined
to encounter at this moment, out of her kitchen
my brother's mother then came calling: What is it?
She looked at the apples of her eyes, her no longer
schoolboys of sons, she saw the swords, the stair upon
which her own blood dripped, the hand on the rail,
the dangling eyeball, the lowered head of
the sacrificial offering, the red hand of her eldest
and halved vision of her youngest son,
and she stood still.

The words are always as
strange and dead as those
fragments and oddments that
the wave casts up on the shore:
I stand in the sea mist
gazing down at the white
words and old bits of wood
and wonder what they were for.

I think that they were not
ever intended to do
what, when we seek to speak,
we believe that they may:
they cannot bear us up
the frothy words and like
wings at the lame foot
lift us out of the clay.

For all the reflections
I call up out of the sea
(they seem to speak as the shell
seems to speak for the sea)
are no more truly here
than the wind weaving sand
into the shapes of things
we think that we know and see.

When in the evening sky
a single star appears
over my head, and the moon
out of cloud lifts its face,
when the white gull turns
or the high plover hovers
to tell me with a cry
I trespass in this place:

What I see, then, with
that cloud my witness is
not shapes of the mind or wind
like the slow rainbowings
of the dolphin's skin as it dies
but, as though from the cloud
I saw my bone walk the shore,
the theology of all things.

The white stones and the old
odd bits of sea blanched wood,
Overstrand and the swinging
lighthouse glimpsed in the mists,
they flash in the prisms and I
believe for a moment I see
the dazzling atoms dancing
in every thing that exists.

The children dance on the shore.
The waves die on the sand.
The spray blows to and fro,
the children dance and die.
What waves are these that dance
with the children on the sand?
I hear them calling, but cannot
hear what it is that they cry.

I neither understand
nor know why I am moved
beyond these words by the
odd bits of bleached wood
cast up on Overstrand
or by the black and twisted
October evening tree
dying beside the road

or by the child of midnight
so deep asleep but still
lost in the corridors
of the mansions of dust,
by any or by all
ceremonial evidence
attesting that we love
simply because we must.

I walk upon Overstrand shore
and the crab at my foot
inscribes praise in the sand.
The wave bursts with glory
because it rises up like
angels out of the sea,
and the dead starfish burns
on Overstrand promontory.

Why do I hear them cry
out from the far side of life,
those forms and impulses
unborn beyond the sky?
Why should they hope and seek
above all else to be?
Tonight on Overstrand
I know for one moment why.

(*In Memory of David Archer*, 1973)

The Ring-a-Roses Tree

What is it that the child
brings to us in both hands
like a bunch of ever
lasting glories or forget me
not that never fade
or daisy chains that net
us all in a ring-a-roses?
It is, I believe, the hope
nothing can extirpate,
that the heart of a stone
still bleeds, still weeps, still
dances along the shore,
still somehow affirms
the metaphysics of dirt,
still feels within the rock
that locked up its own springs
fountains not yet divined.
At the grave of poisoned
intellectual energy
where the intelligence
surrounded with its huge
and hopeless trophies lies,
the cup of suicide still
clutched in a clever hand,
there I have seen the child
step forward, orphaned, and
cast smiling into that grave
its wretched little ring
of rose and daisy. Out
of that overgrown and
undergrowth grave where now
belief and faith like maggots

mock on the rotten bone,
out of that dirt and out
of that stone heart I see
dying upward like hope
the ring-a-roses tree.

(*Dialogues, Etc.,* 1976)

from Villa Stellar

I

Why the white oxen? Simply because they are gone.
May they haunt the bright springs of Clitumnus for ever.
But I too have watched their delicate lolloping into
and out of those marzipan springs welling up like the melting of
rainbows
among emerald meadows painted afresh every morning
and seen Renoir's blood drip from their horns in the evening
and known that I was not dreaming. Now they are really gone.
Only
the proprietor's dog sleeps outside the café at noonday
and I speak in vain for the dead. The small temple so plainly
forgotten a mile further down the new highway
that in the rain a long distance lorry driver idly
supposes it nothing better than a derelict public lavatory,
there, there a dead friend and I sat sipping Frascati together
and watched the great white bullocks unwinding ribbons
of water like rainbows from around their ankles, and we know
when we see
the funeral phantasmagoria of what will never return.
So may the great white oxhead that sleeps undisturbed by even
Propertius or the susurration of a hundred poplar trees in the
evening
haunt these springs of Clitumnus for ever.

XI

Yes, that corner fireplace in the cottage by Lake Nemi
how it flickers its flames among then and now to
illuminate these images like trophies. I see the arbutus
bough hung like a pair of bronze antlers over the mantelpiece
catching occasional and fiery gleams out of shadows and

for an instant transfiguring a broken branch into
the Golden Bough of Diana. And why not, since with my
own hand I broke that branch off the tree that time had elected
to plant where she once slept at her altar and
where the murderer could never sleep? Why is
that wood sacred? It is sacred because, if you walk there
you will perceive that this wood and the handmirror lake
happen to be haunted by a presence of human dereliction
that walks there as though we might be gods again.

XXVI

But is there a story to tell? There is always a story
of people who seek among streets and the dead ends of the mind
for what they have lost
as they looked for the house and the homeward angel.
What are you doing here among the wrack and ruin of a
hope that the hope still mourns for? Each of us lives
in a mansion constructed of mirrors that reflect only
the emptiness of all rooms save the chamber of wax
effigies who died for us. What I wrong when
I write these lines is condolence to these dead
who do not know they are dead and therefore continue
to sit around in the catacombs of my days and drink coffee
as though death was life, which, for all I know,
it may well be. Then Adam may rhapsodize in the
mouth of the worm and the sleepers make love in the grave
and I meet again as I enter
the lily-wreathed bedroom
an I who sits there believing he is still breathing.

To all appearances the life serene:
tea in the afternoon with two old ladies; talk
of this and that, and who and who have been
seen arm in arm on a Sunday walk;
how well the new tomato plant; what who said
when the old cow died; why the milk was sour.
He sat and chatted with them by the hour
until the time came to go in to bed.

The floorboards of the ballroom open up.
The flames. The pillar of. Who are you. Blood.
Something is burning somewhere. Waltz of Death.
The fire. I am I am. The flesh. The cup.
He would start screaming if he only could.
I feel the fangs and smell the stinking breath.

XLVII

Hand of my hand, rest.
Heart of my heart, sleep.
Bright eye of childhood count
the lambs and not the sheep:
may the shepherd keep
a watch over your bed
till every lamb and you
rest a dreaming head.

The monsters of the day
have fled to other fields,
and now the mothering one
her milk of moonlight yields
and the great hunter wields
his wonders in the sky:

may all the monsters of
night and the nightmare fly.

From the foal and from
the kitten, child and kid
as they dream within
the eye and shuttered lid
our shoddy world is hid:
may a Mary of dreams
show them it is not
as monstrous as it seems.

LII

Now this bloody war is over
no more soldiering for me.
I can hear the angel in the kitchen
washing up the crockery for tea,
and down the lane the donkeys and the children
splashing through the puddle by the tree
and the daffodils that should have died in April
ostentatiously continuing to be,
so now this bloody war is over
no more soldiering for me.

Us dead are up and dancing in the garden,
us dead are throwing parties every night
and the destiny of man is with the children
daubing every bleeding elephant dead white
and us dead men and the children in the garden
are dancing hand in hand such a helluva saraband
that the Church and State in bed think it's thunder overhead
as the children and us dead dance through the night.

The children are gone. The holiday is over.
Outside it is Fall. Inside it is so
quiet that the silence seems inclined to
talk to itself. They will not recover
the summer of seventy-seven again, even
though they become, in turn, their own children.

I sit in my sixty odd years and wonder
how often before in this old house a man has
sat thinking of what is now, and what was.
But can it serve a serious purpose to ponder
upon the imponderable? There, there beyond a
fall glimmers the long-lost garden.

That garden where we, too, as in a spell
stared eye into dazed eye and did not see
that suddenly the holy day was over,
the flashing lifeguard, the worm in the tree,
the glittering of the bright sword as it fell,
and the gate closing for all time to be.

(*Villa Stellar*, 1978)

from Sacred Elegies [V]

I

These errors loved no less than the saint loves arrows
Repeat, Love has left the world. He is not here.
O God, like Love revealing yourself in absence
So that, though farther than stars, like Love that sorrows
In separation, the desire in the heart of hearts
To come home to you makes you most manifest.
The booming zero spins as his halo where
Ashes of pride on all the tongues of sense
Crown us with negatives. O deal us in our deserts
The crumb of falling vanity. It is eucharist.

II

Everyone walking everywhere goes in a glow
Of geometrical progression, all meteors, in praise:
Hosannas on the tongues of the dumb shall raise
Roads for the gangs in chains to return to
God. They go hugging the traumas like halleluias
To the bodies that earn this beatitude. The Seven
Seas they crowd like the great sailing clippers,
Those homing migrants that, with their swallow-like sails set,
Swayed forward along the loneliness that opposed,
For nothing more than a meeting in heaven.

III

Therefore all things, in all three tenses,
Alone like the statue in an alcove of love,
Moving in obedient machinery, sleeping
Happy in impossible achievements, keeping
Close to each other, because the night is dark;
The great man dreaming on the stones of circumstances,
The small wringing hands because rocks will not move:
The beast in its red kingdom, the star in its arc:
O all things, therefore, in shapes or in senses,
Know that they exist in the kiss of his Love.

IV

Incubus, Anæsthetist with glory in a bag,
Foreman with a sweatbox and a whip. Asphyxiator
Of the ecstatic. Sergeant with a grudge
Against the lost lovers in the park of creation,
Fiend behind the fiend behind the fiend behind the
Friend. Mastodon with mastery, monster with an ache
At the tooth of the ego, the dead drunk judge:
Wheresoever Thou art our agony will find Thee
Enthroned on the darkest altar of our heartbreak
Perfect. Beast, brute, bastard. O dog my God!

(*Eros in Dogma*, 1944)

Anno Domini

— at a time of bankers
    to exercise a little charity;
at a time of soldiers
    to cultivate small gardens;
at a time of categorical imperatives
    to guess about clouds;
at a time of politicians
    to trust only to children and demigods.
And from those who occupy seats of power
    to turn, today, away
without incurring permanent reprisals.
    When the instruments of torture
are paraded in public places
    permit us to transmute them,
somehow, into ploughshares.
    When the tribulations of some tribes, or persons,
seem, as so often, to exceed a reasonable allotment,
    condescend, superior, to examine fate
and make sure that its machinery has not gone wrong.
    When those who deserve little more than
a severe whipping, wake up to a morning of pink
    champagne and strawberries,
visit them, surely, with one moment of retribution
    and slight indigestion. Expunge
from the punishment book of the frivolous
    those impositions incurred for singing at funerals;
and to the hopelessly optimistic
    award, if you will, a few kisses. When diagrams
dictate to our sympathetic systems, and the operation
    of stars deludes us that
it is wholly inauspicious,
    cheer us then, O Leda, with a kind

and silent light. Lord of the raddled and the penurious
  impute to those who have failed
no more serious an error than that of
  caring too much about success;
promote those who sit patiently twiddling
  their thumbs on benches, and let
even those who love Persian cats see, sometimes,
  that dogs are ours also.
Pardon if you will the thief or orphan or me
  stealing a meal from Babylon,
and the prince who absconds with the funds
  for a better reason. And let not,
let not everything we do
  become a final farewell.
Magister, legislate for us when on your
  circuit even we the guilty smirk in
our knowledge that greed motivates also
  the Grand Inquisitor with his bouquet of
feudal flowers, let alone the invidious
  putative I.
Supplant those who grow old with those who
  only grow roses, and let the Spanish
sun jockey all Black Princes back again into
  Aquitainian towers. Where dust storms prevail
let your face, Moses, appear in the mirage
  of Lebanon, speaking the one and
only word we can hear. Not by trial and error
  delegate to us those sorrows that rise from
our own trials and errors
  but dispose the Russian snows kindly towards us
so that they fall as warm as
  astra can. When on our tigers we
ride into Afghanistan
  loud with bullroarers,

call to our mind the fate of that Limerick girl
    who rode a tiger from Niger
but only one way. After those thunderstorms visit us
    in your most tender of forms,
the sky serene. And after eleven plagues
    as the white nurse come among the
seven sleeping survivors, and after all wars
    for a day withdraw from us
for only then may we see
    what it is we have done.
Strike the lamb dumb
    if it should Ego sing
and poleaxe the bull
    if it should bully the lamb
or bugger the powerless. When
    the knife of kisses excoriates
the flesh that it loves the best
    let the knife and lover be forgiven
and even perhaps the flesh.
    Hide, if you must, your face
from the homicidal maniac
    so that, though blind, he sees
you are not gone, but only
    like the moon turned away
from the crime which we cannot
    as yet understand, but must,
blind mystery of justice,
    believe to be somehow involved
in the exonerating epicycles of your will.

Will you also withdraw from those who
    carrying placards declaring
their total devotion to
    your service, proceed to demand

the death of their friends and even
      your enemies? Remove from
the crawling infant that instrument
      neither Heisenberg nor
Max Planck would ever dream
      of introducing into
a nursery, that little
      planetary construction of coloured
balls that seems likely to
      serve as our one and only
commemorative memorial? Among stars
      do I hear you whisper outside
their laboratories that yours yes
      yours was the first
but not the last big bang?
      For have you not, least hostile
of all possible hosts,
      amply provided us with
so much provender that,
      given the rope, and the hope,
what could we do save eat
      that bit of bread, loop up
the hanging hope, and trust
      in the end that the rope
would bear us up? Not
      no, not the belief.
I believe the belief
      fell from the lectern as
we sat and listened.
      But we forgot the words
and mistook those notes
      that fell, for, perhaps, music.
When the little ones walk in
      the old garden what godsend

will descend upon them? Flowers?
     Or, astronomer, am I in error
and will what falls on them crush
     these kids like the grinding mills
and enormous prisms that turn
     so slowly, the altering stones and
looming epicycles —
     will these descend upon them?
They will, for these are truly
     the huge masonry of
collapsing belief. And so arraign but not
     too mildly those who purvey
arid principles among us
     as though they proffered us flowers.
Better than any belief
     the hope that survives the death
of formal dogma. Then
     on the day of showers
we depart on prolonged picnics.
     So my beloved bare
your throat to me and watch
     Absalom flash with kisses:
then let the old vulture do
     its deadly best to sing
and the corybantic drunk
     see visions of a blue
Fra Angelican clarity.
     Turn your hand not away
from the wilfully unemployed
     because they employ the state
as not from those whom the state
     only too wilfully employs. Mitigate
the frenzy of the erotic system
     in the heart of those who outlive

their time; transmute the ferocity
     of the fanatic into
a purpose conscious of moral proportion;
     a little tenderly flagellate
the flagellators, and lead back to the way
     (are we not all him?) the crossed
roads of the pervert. When
     at chance moments clouds of
change seem to do nothing
     but darken the landscape in which
we necessarily labour
     let a little illumination
from inexplicable sources
     descend on Brueghelian fields.
Will you, at times, momentarily
     modify the optics of providence
so that some of us may see
     what best to do next? As when
the sleeping statesman dreams of the colour red
     and yet awakens with roses in his hands?
What tree will you eventually permit
     the uneaten apple of Eve to grow again on?

Then to whom save the prince of darkness
     shall we sacrifice a thousand
electric light bulbs? To whom save Machiavelli immolate
     a generation of truthful computers?
When the moon shines a construction
     of crystal and white lies appears in the garden
to commemorate all assassinated facts
     and the whitewashed elephants of
social hypocrisy. To whom else, then,
     save our rather unsavoury selves
shall we sacrifice the self-agonizing god?

At a time of saints to encourage counterfeiters.
At a time of millionaire soccer stars
    to knit gloves for starving golliwogs.
Correct, O director, in time the fugitive clock
    that ticks a little too fast into
the future because it is sick both of the present
    and the forfeited past. Alleviate
the conscience of the deaf piano tuner
    who knows he knows no way to recognize
the perfect note, and knows, therefore,
    all notes must be imperfect.
Upon bad-tempered and hardened argufiers play
    the sprinkling hosepipe of
the heavenly humour that
    gave us the aardvark and the ballooning
hippopotamus. Vary in municipal gardens
    those strict arrangements of flowers
that remind us of German philosophers.

Impeach all presidents who seek
    to preside over private persons, and favour
all vendors of black ice cream.
    From congenital enemies remove
their passports, hobnailed boots and
    birth certificates so
that they think they are
    for the time being two quite
congenial persons. Comfort the brood
    of nine puppies with no foreknowledge
of a dog's life and let the caterwauling
    of microphones not abash serenaders.
For who – was it you? – made bleed and weep
    the laws of arithmetic as they nailed out
humanitas limb by limb like Jewish crucifixions on

the hackenkreuz? Will you answer me?
I will retreat to archipelagos where
    responses to these cloudy questions stalk
up and down proudly like red-stockinged
    flamingos, and in the air such a plucking
of stringed instruments that the shipwrecked
    philosopher thinks that he hears
the psalteries of spiritual vision.
    Accord, then, to the stone-deaf, somehow,
an interpretation of these dialogues
    with which rocks and stones and trees
and particularly water
    seek continually to answer us.
Will your hand hesitate before
    it locks the undertaker's casket
on the unrepentant old lag, or the couple who,
    having nicer things, as they feel, to do
arrive a bit late for their funeral?
    Extend, that is, if you will, latitude
to those who steal little things, like, on Sundays,
    an hour of love. And to Arcadia lead
those among us, who, sleeping alone in suburbia,
    dream of goatherds and that
far-off unfabled Korya of honey-tongued brandy
    and brown bell-hung young goats
whickering in morning mountains.
    When homeward we
turn from distant Argos, grant
    that one blade of Agamemnon's
golden fields may somehow
    still tick in our memory or
whisper of honour to an attentive
    tympanum. May all Mycenaean
mountains remind us that over

the darkest of caves and crimes
as over the violent lives of violent men
    the great white clouds of summer, like
compassion may sometimes, sooner
    or later, pass in a silent
propitiation. The birds fly daily
    out of such places as though
they brought from the haunts of the ruined
    ages news that the dead and the deserving
still dream in their famous tombs
    undisturbed by recurring
nightmares of the demi-urge,
    American engineers or the money spider.
As, over that ossified structure of
    intellectual dogma, the ziggurat
of scientific conviction,
    (the dogma that fact is
final, when we know it in truth
    to be no more than one story
of the Babbling Tower we
    astrologize in) over that
Manhattan of the mind let a sunrise
    or a shepherding sunset play
its many colours until
    all actual knowledge looks
like what it seems to be:
    a kaleidoscope inside
a magic lantern. For are there not
    always other shores and other
further marvellous islands
    where invisible flora
and fauna perform in their
    . long-hidden gardens, where Lilith
may well awaken one brilliant morning

again? Where are you leading me?
To that railway station, over-
    grown with fireweed, long-abandoned,
derelict, the signals dislocated,
    the sleepers uprooted, the name
by time erased, and the lines rusting
    after red rain? The station
without a crossing, where the mind, alighting,
    finds that it has arrived
in a place that exists alas
    no longer. Where the announcements
hang heavy with dead ideas,
    and consolations of the exhausted
conscience rot in flowerbeds
    like last year's roses.

In a time of fashionable evangelists
    to retire to small vegetable allotments;
in a time of doctors and aristocratic actresses
    to eavesdrop on the dialogues of worms;
in a time of national anthems and brass bands
    to conduct rigorous callisthenics for corpses;
in a time of bald-headed administrators
    to erect beribboned maypoles and
encourage cardsharpers; in a time of Scandinavian
    architecture and pornography to wrestle
with incubi and succubi; in a time of magicians and water diviners
    to remember, nevertheless, that we can fly.
From moralistic and political trials
    allow us O lord chief justice to draw
our own biased conclusions without
    fear of the bell the book or the final
abomination. Persecute the persecutors, counsel the counsellors
    and police the police.

Arraign the arraigners, mock the mockers and reform
      the reformers. Among
the shenanigans of moral foxes, O MFH,
      release the hounds of Here and Hereafter.
Modify the laws of cause and effect
      so that not even those guilty
of failed practical jokes like the Jesuits
      spend too long a time in Coventry.
Will you award a candle to those who whistle
      in valium dark? To those going under
for the third time, the lame, the dumb
      and any one else whom Seneca
might have thought monstrous,
      to them cast a rope or the branch
of a holly tree. Help us
      avoid a void. Nor let the moral philosopher
drive us with whips into the practice of
      moral philosophy, nor the humanitarian
with a discipline drive us into venal
      love of one another, but mitigate
the myopia we suffer from whenever
      we seek to perceive the working
of your gardener William in
      the common or garden. On the
day when you speak shall I not hear but see?
      In a time of vipers I will show
my sign. But if I walk down a street
      in which I see no one else at all
but hear the footsteps and feel the presence
      of a second person walking behind me,
shall I say, nevertheless, that I am alone,
      or shall I confess that
I am subject to hallucinations?
      What is the logic, Aquinas,

of this confusing image? All that I
    think I perceive is rational and
conditioned by laws of
    responsibility and reason: this,
in the simple sense, is reality. But those
    footsteps persist and that presence
continues to follow or to precede me.

The Pyrrhic victories of the rational
    surround us on all sides with
scenes of violence, carnage and
    barbaric triumphal arches:
but somewhere in the mirage-ridden
    hinterland of the spirit,
among the hallucinations and delusions
    of that desert (which some of us
happily believe does not exist at all),
    somewhere there the crucifixion
of Adam is continually committed. I am that I am
    nailed up anew daily.
What are you looking for in this degraded
    landscape? Not for what is so
mysteriously there: for you are looking for
    what you have lost there
what you have done and won there
    but you are no longer looking for
what is and was and always will be so
    everlastingly there:
a dead-drunk conscience weeping
    over the mad and ravished Psyche.

In a time of hypochondriacal philosophers
    children play happily in public gardens;
in a time of statistics
    anarchy denudes herself of the seventh veil;

and in a time of magistrates
    criminals invent new crimes;
in a time of hedonists and belly dancers
    wise men draw the blinds and bolt the doors.
In a time of journalists most decent things
    acquire the gift of invisibility;
in a time of death all of us suddenly
    and miraculously discover that we are alive.
Sometimes favour, if you will, the arrogant
    of intellect with an odour as of
unknowable roses, and the proud man
    with a pair of unreliable braces.
Upon autumn lakes scatter the feathers
    of foolish patriots in foreign fields,
and bring to the beds of those who suffer
    a benign sister with a handful of poppies
not for remembrance, but to forget.
    As to Arcadia also
I bring that overloaded old bag of the ego
    covered with coloured stickers
enumerating the travelogue of vanity and
    expensive guilt, to find
that forgotten poppy also
    growing among those mountains
that still hide the dithyrambical
    and deathless Pan.
But can I confide to you, mediator,
    the fear I fear I fear
faced with the sleight of hand you perform
    upon the ascending spheres and even
upon every day and the common place?
    As when rain chooses to fall upon
fields that need it, or the insane sun
    declines the whim to fry us like onions

or as the star-fished sea
     keeps to its beds and basins on
the classroom globe.
     These things can be seen, I know,
as subject to simple laws. And these are the mysteries
     I find myself facing with a kind of tremble.
For, as I see it, these natural laws
     comprise the only evidence I can perceive
of a superior purpose working
     up through all things. Thus when the old
tree falls in October wind (as no less
     the sparrow's feather) it falls because
it was ordained to fall not by the laws
     of Time or Newton, but by the will
that upon all things has imposed its natural
     and even supernatural purposes.
As in the recurring seven-veiled dance of
     physics and the conundrum
of prime numbers' *perpetuum mobile* or
     that diastole and systole at
the heart of things, the quixotic quanta, or
     the principle that seeks to teach us
a little intellectual humility,
     the will-o'-the-wisp perversity of
the hide-and-seek neutrino. It is then that
     though very darkly we might see
what your wish or your will may be:
     that, no less than
the madman killing or shark with a red jaw
     or the assassination of photographs or
the avalanche collapsing over
     Obermann villages or the entire
universe trying to find out
     how wide it is, so we obey your will

when we obey your image.
    And tremble, then, at the mystery of evil.
Let who will lay upon the stone
    of the run-over child a wreath
inscribed: *Dei voluntas*. I will not, for there is a mystery here
    not given to any, yet, to understand.
The printed shadows of Hiroshima, do they
    point their evaporated hands at us
or you? How could it have been you?
    This is a thing so evil that
it could have come from nowhere save a mind
    capable of inventing the idea of evil.
We are, professor, out of joint with the purpose
    of your work; whatever that point may be,
we are out of joint with it. You know.
    Newman knew. We know. 'The human race
is implicated in some aboriginal
    calamity.' This is the mystery, this
calamity that, snakes coiled in its cloudy hair,
    sits on the great tripod of past, present
and what future, hypnotizing the dove
    with catastrophic images of the possible.
And so all the stories that little children play-act
    on their picnics or by winter firesides,
tales of the Polyphemi–Frankenstein monsters
    that waken up and eat us, this is what you
doctor have done. Here is the mad creature
    you have created. Have you built your own
murder into the marvellous faculties
    we use because we possess?
What does this shambling machine whisper
    as it crawls and stumbles among rocks and ruins,
its clockwork eyes clouded with self-hate, its
    terminals cancerous, wetware and wordwrite

alphanumeric, phonemed,
     automatic forks pick-
ing up isotopes, robotics utterly grouched,
     the reproductive generator hanging
down like an obsolete decoration, the
     anthropic spirit skinnered, the
enigma cybernized,
     the circuit of the nervous system worn
to a nexus of Freudian wires,
     what does this shambling machine whisper
when it encounters, down the dark path,
     halfway through a Black Forest, of
a midwinter midnight,
     the huge god riding on a dead white horse?
What, what does it whisper?
     'I am a man'?

Arbiter of dreams open my sleep-walking
     eye upon scenes I cannot recognize
when in the morning I wake among nightmares. Let me see
     some humane minds still uncorrupted, some
good men not angling for
     even bigger fishes and some
women not cultivating Chinese little fingernails
     and poisonous flower power,
some farmers not ashamed of the name George, some
     doctors prepared to prescribe for ailments
not amended by penicillin, some gardeners providing
     a herb we seem to have lost, the *herba sacra*;
some couples actually thinking of truly
     mutual pleasures; some children
playing games without guns and some priests
     practically praying. Some birds in nests
not for sale and at evening some edible browsers

grazing at grass; some small kingdoms
not constructing sub-atomic megakills; some
        cities not gourmandizing spaghetti junctions;
some gardens growing a little wild in
        southern seaside townships; some
African elephants in Africa;
        some sunrises to which we may awaken
without the mind clouded by those poisoned
        vapours that now hang over every
mushroom field. But 'Complaint',
        said a holy man, 'is sin.' Those mists
of the morning slowly disperse as
        the light climbs higher; invalids eventually
throw off sheets and step out into
        everyday rituals; overgrown even
battlefields after a time. Through a window
        in the gutted mansion
a flowering bush sooner or later
        pushes its optimistic blossoms
and from haunted lives one day
        the ghouls have fled, leaving
the kitchen just habitable; in the waste land
        a gypsy family has set up a homestead,
and in the derelict heart a worm of hope
        is still found breathing under
a broken hearth stone. 'All Nature, inasmuch as
        it is Nature, is good.' For, somewhere,
hidden in its darkest heartland,
        down in the germinal and platonic
cave, dreaming in the sea, cradled in graves as
        sometimes glimpsed in clouds,
the origins of the possible speak to us
        of what we might do if
in this once heavenly setting we

recollected fabled Arcadia
and why we lost it.

   At a time of conundrums and rabies
to inhale oxygen and to evoke
      supernatural precedents. At a time
of tubercular novelists and pot-bellied champions
      to sharpen pencils and rig up
large tents for boy scouts and chimpanzees.
   At a time of bad apples and short circuits
and popular comics to manufacture winter
      socks and encourage cricketers. At
a time of multiplying hysterics
      to collect tears and Jordan water.
Consecrate, master of ceremonies,
      the faithless mind to a faithful purpose
and turn the conscience of India towards
      social constructions superior to Taj Mahals
and the Christian missionary to
      a prettier position and the Mao Tse
Marxist to moments of fallibility and forgiveness.
   Allow dogs to survive in a world
from which they will undoubtedly soon be excluded
      and the whale to wallow about,
like us, for a little while longer.
   To their domestic hearth let
all Argonauts return with their
      cameras intact and a few sentimental
mementoes; pacify those who seek
      to trouble fresh waters where the famished
hopelessly fish; load the wagons of harvest
      gatherers with all sorts of fruit
including a real cornucopia; put down those
      equine statues of field marshals who

mobilized, so they supposed, armies of digits; and
    degrade all invigilators
because they trust no one; let
    fall upon the Just some summer sunshine
as it does upon the Unjust; fend off
    fire from the playing babe and attend,
dominie, those hundreds and thousands of us
    who do not know the right thing to do.
Or is it all, really,
    just for the birds? Then may we
learn a little from them. But consider, Paraclete,
    the dove, devoted advocate of Venus,
animula, vagula, blandula,
    that Picassoid pledger of peace,
does not this pure carnivore,
    cave-mouthed like Chronos, devour
its own fledgling children
    in the parsonage dovecote? Can
we appeal with any expectation of answers
    to our local and more modest deities?
They are, after all, your higher executives,
    branch managers, as it were, possessing
some administrative powers. What of
    the jesus prayer or the curative
operations of oriental mantra?

What of the long history of
    small miracles at the Aesculapian
tabernacle? You, Jahweh,
    still, still asleep on Sinai? No,
they do not respond to these
    supplications addressed upward by
those whose devotion also dedicates itself
    to even dimmer demigods like money

or Lenin or the demon of
        social democracy or Liberty or
any of the other parthenogenetical idols
        a cynical fancy flatters. These
deities sit around like
        museum plaster statues
allowing us all to cleanse their clay feet
        from vast lachrymatories
that copiously overflow now.
        And the little dog laughs to see such fun
and the fish runs away with the moon.

Illusions have spoken the truth in obscure language
        about matters we cannot speak of at all.
I mean the death of the heart
        that does not know it is dead because
it continues to suffer
        and like a headless chicken stalks around
bleeding Chinese ideograms signifying Pity
        down the garden path. As winter
fix the variable and valuable
        opinions of water, and the variant
mind that slips away down any
        conduit or convenience, fix it
with fortitude towards the purpose
        for which it must run up hill.
If certain colours of the spectrum
        and several notes of the diapason
remain beyond our perception
        why not several modes of existence
beyond our sublunary comprehension?
        We have yet to invent the instruments
capable of entering these spheres.

I have looked, as have so many others,
	In so many catacombs and hecatombs
that echo only with our futile footsteps,
	for you, the absconded. Who have gone
from all the places, gone from the grave and fountain,
	from the cave of the mind, gone from the shrine
and the forgotten shibboleth, gone from the fallen and
	shit-littered temple, the *pissoir* tabernacle,
gone from the infested altar and
	the screaming cathedrals,
left only cold air and the zero booming about us,
	gone from the heart where once
you surely broke bread in the human house
	without a sup of sorrow, gone from those
transfigured seas where an amoeba rose and
	monstrously prophesied revolution over
Darwinian waters —
	so many in so many clefts of the mind
seek even now. I have found nothing. Nothing.
	Not so little as on the rock
an Adam footprint, or the mind overturned
	to commemorate your passing.
Only, in the void an invisible
	alcove enshrining the huge sibyl
of your absence. Singing lamb, sweet Pascal,
	not the god of Abraham or Isaac,
not the god of philosophers and scholars,
	not even in the end the X one, but
whatever or whoever it is that
	we were invented to venerate.
Behind all the altars and the entablatured
	tabernacles, behind the mantra and the
unfolding mandelion, behind the mandala and the
	May *magnificat*, the *sanctum sanctum sanctorum*,

beyond even the void, the *ideos* and the *logos*,
     behind all that can be spoken or imagined,
is it really there, the one thing
     we cannot ever know?

At a time of enigmas and pandoras,
     of treetop browsing question marks and labyrinths
where the faceless in wheelchairs regularly
     perform their daily round,
at a time of asking, knowing
     there are no even unsatisfactory answers,
at a time of hopeless appellations,
     to eavesdrop on the conversations of
canonical photographers, to memorize
     the regulations of suburban public gardens,
to calculate odd eclipses, and to operate
     mechanisms imposing order on the winds.
At a time of absolute silence
     to listen to its orations.

Come home, fisherman, come home, come home,
     leave the long-dead Aegean and old Arnold's
far colder sea to sleep without bad dreams
     wandering over the surface of this failure
of all faith, our truly dead sea. No flying fish now
flitter over philosophies, no dolphins dive
     down through the glooms of doubt to
find drowned mythologies; the blindfold sirens
     shriek only in hysterics, and
great argosies of ideas and archangels lie
     burning and broken and rolling
on the flim-flam rocks. And the heart –
     crying along the shores and years it runs
echoing again and ululating it
     mourns as it flies,

the suicidal lamentation of the god
    for the dying man.

Accord us, star of the sea, one ray like
    the X of a crime. Visit
the infant of strangled human innocence with
    a kiss of life out of
the flower's mouth.
    Star of the spirit delude us
with your beautiful hallucinations
    before we wholly believe
in our own futile illusions.
    At a time of terror and ecclesiastical
massacres to erect charitable
    institutions and schools
for penitential suicides. At a time of intolerance
    and the decimation of marsupials
to light candles in subversive
    chapels and to bury the dead
with tomahawks in their hands.
    At a time of coldblooded calculators
and rigorous bigots to plant
    druidical oaks and cultivate
impious Cagliostros. At a time of orations
    to listen to silences. Lead
homeward also the circuitous
    interlect wandering lost in the
arroyas of Arizona like a mad
    guilt-ridden somnambulist;
castigate the hypocritical atom; liberate
    from its liberties that chained
giant, noetic conscience. Let
    matter forgive Lord Rutherford
and light Albert Einstein. Militate

against the military and
liquidate the liquidators. Upon all
    altruists in South America
allow an agape to shine, for
    in the aviaries of the spirit
all birds, even the decapitated,
    can sing, and in the green summer
of the compassionate mind
    the myxomatosized rabbit run wild
again and on the harps of gold Pythagoras
    even Mongolian children play
psychotic paeans and poems of praise.
    Among melancholy mansions blind
nightingales elect to regale us. Under polluted
    waterfalls where we have sat
paralysed by the loud laws of acquadynamics
    we have bathed tomorrow morning
under a sun of gentler dispensations,
    and from long-derelict underground junctions
departed on journeys to remote and mythological Jordans.
    Some of us have even been visited
as we knelt in silent shrines
    by charming criminals; to others of us
bunches of spring flowers
    sometimes appeared in autumn and
to others again from dirty dustbins
    the poetic phoenix like
a rocket arisen. For, ferociously
    apparelled in flayed human flesh,
indestructible ideals
    have walked among us, slinging
blood from Struwwelpeter's
    scissored fingers. Divers have
descended into Tuscaroras where

        our idols lie dumb-foundered and
brought dazzling up to us again
        marvellous images, more
memorable than mermaids, images
        marbled with memories
of moral vision,
        like dripping statues of
the heroic mythos.
        Where chance encounters
occurred between unfriendly
        children, there societies
of Miltonic birds have rhapsodized
        not only to commemorate
such occasions but also
        to teach us praise.
Sometimes these high-flying
        effigies have pursued us over
dark parks and vast ages
        and black waters, begging us
with broken voices never
        never to forget them. I have
sat down to breakfast with
        a lost cause and found that it
was neither lost, nor a cause.
        It was merely everyone
looking for everyone else to forgive us
        before we all die. Near the world's end
there is an old elm tree
        where this seemed sometimes to happen
but ten tons of Time fell
        out of a war and only
the shades remain. I lean my ear
        to the cellar wall
and hear the mad underground

river roaring in flood
laden with killed chairs,
corpses, the debris of graves,
dismembered limbs and memories
that toss like the horns
of drowned cattle out of the floods
and I know that I hear
the torrents of anno domini.
This, then, is a scene
of many defeats by moonlight
when every word was a deep
dishonourable wound and every
act a betrayal and
every idea an evasion
of what should but could
therefore never be done.
I speak of this always
present war that none of
the living ever survive
and of which the victor
is always the ritual victim:
when, to vanquish the viper
we begin to slither and coil,
or into the bully to beat
battling bravadoes turn.
But how can any lines measure
such immeasurably sad times
save in terms of blood-red
revolutions of the heart
or of poppies that poison
even our lachrymae christi?
The interior of this cathedral
fills with a fear no candle
can seem to illuminate

and no evening sunlight
a little tenderly relieve
and no ceremonies sanctify
and no word speak for. This
testament is constructed
out of old bones and discarded
razor blades and
the stained-glass days of the dead.

As anarchy come among us
when we sit studying the
hypocritical formalities of
injustice in the Maze
as once in Kilmainham
MacSwiney; as mercy
come among us
when we ride holy cows
over those buried up to the neck
in doubt or debt; as pity
come among us
when we peruse newspapers,
the lives of the aged or
those notes sung by
battered brides; as justice
come among us if
we close our eyes upon
Sten guns, millionaires' yachts or
the machinations of intemperate fanatics;
as caritas come among us
when we cross the deserted
Arabias between us all;
and as hope attend us when
we stand on the high
diving-board over

an empty future.
Between summer and autumn forbid
    an Ides of March to re-enter
as again between winter and spring;
    between intoxicated friends
disallow the fractionate rocks;
    between now and then introduce
one traumatic moment
    of mutual forgiveness;
between lovers discourage the growth
    of obscene hybrids, and between the
rogations of grief, water
    those lilies that dance. Conceal
from the cripple all instruments
    (such as the violin) shaped
like the bodies of demigods;
    show to the wild horse
the fate of the Otto cycle;
    hide in obscurities
our brilliant flashes of ignis fatuus or
    the putrescent intelligence;
reveal to those who truly forget themselves
    new vistas of
henceforth immaculate genealogies. Where decay
    kingdoms abandoned by kings
encourage the hegemony of
    that hardy perennial
the Athenian demon.
    Where the domestic cat
revives the luxors of
    pharaonic Egypt may
sphinxes with colossal queries
    trouble all feline dreams
of political power.

Where houses of doubt and snow abound
arrange that a mild sun very faintly shines
    every day. Let us cease to fear dust
and remember that even clay
    feet walk around in a world
that every May Day restores.
    At a time of fire-flecked dawns
rancid milk bottles and outmoded medallions,
    some slowly swimming martyrs bring
messages to those marooned
    on unfamiliar foreshores. Allegories
arrive by electric trains daily, and,
    met by meteorologists,
lug from their bags
    documents attesting that they also started
from the Finland Station. And that also
    they arrive armed.
At a time of reviewers, Chinese vulgarians and
    methodical universes,
to speculate on the population of anthills,
    to retire to the Turkish baths, and
to inflate Montgolfier balloons.

Teach us not to despair on Tuesdays
    when all things seem to recede
into temporal mirrors, and
    cover over with dust sheets
those effigies that ululate in the
    abandoned mansions. Mark time
not with a red cross but a hyaline;
    draw from the mad man's eye
the beam that blinds it and let
    the dreams of Aphasia attend
those in mental institutions. Open over the soul's

appalling apertures
bridges like Saarinen wings
　　　and to those who are reduced to
the circumstantial lie
　　　allow a little latitude.

Let ghosts walk in Battersea Park
　　　without dreading an earthly encounter,
and rectify all the errors we make
in our golden account books. Allow
　　　us to sit down at open-air tables
without observing the dawn of
　　　the Dies Irae, or the clock
at last striking midnight. (Why do cupidons
　　　with gold wings loop garlands
in the air over those who dislike
　　　all children? Why do those
who love roses possess gangrened fingers,
　　　and why will the heroic salmon
never learn circumspection?
　　　What carpenter can construct
doors that open only to our good angel? What
　　　statesman listens to the dying sighs
of the white giants?)
　　　The snows of yesterday have returned
to those clouds from which they will fall
　　　tomorrow disguised as summer and
one day the seas will part and from the fissure
　　　Orpheus rise up festooned
with telephone wires to teach us
　　　the triumph of the incommunicable.
Why are heroism and devotion like
　　　great works of art? Because
they have no object beyond themselves?

Why do poets stand around
like telegraph poles? Because
    all they can do is pass on messages?
At a time of bankers
    to exercise a little charity –

(*Anno Domini*, 1983)

To Whom Else

Had I more carefully cultivated the Horatian pentameter, then
this verse would live longer in your remembrance than
things being what they are, I suppose, it briefly will.
Or do I think these verses may survive you, and, well,
do I really care? I do not give a damn.
For I know that if you read them you will condemn
them simply because they were made by that over
devoted zealot who was once, not briefly, your lover.

(*Street Ballads*, 1992)